The Turn to Industry
Forging a Proletarian Party

ALSO BY JACK BARNES

BOOKS & PAMPHLETS

The Clintons' Anti-Working-Class Record (2016)

Are They Rich Because They're Smart? Class, Privilege, and Learning Under Capitalism (2016)

Malcolm X, Black Liberation, and the Road to Workers Power (2009)

Cuba and the Coming American Revolution (2007)

The Changing Face of US Politics (2002)

Their Trotsky and Ours (2002)

The Working Class and the Transformation of Learning (2000)

Capitalism's World Disorder (1999)

Malcolm X Talks to Young People (1969)

FROM THE PAGES OF 'NEW INTERNATIONAL'

Capitalism's Long Hot Winter Has Begun (2005)

Our Politics Start with the World (2005)

US Imperialism Has Lost the Cold War (1998)

The Opening Guns of World War III (1991)

Politics of Economics: Che Guevara and Marxist Continuity (1991)

The Fight for a Workers and Farmers Government in the US (1985)

COLLECTIONS AND INTRODUCTIONS

Tribunes of the People and the Trade Unions (2019)

Teamster Rebellion/Dobbs (2004)

The History of American Trotskyism/Cannon (2002)

The Eastern Airlines Strike/E. Mailhot (1991)

FBI on Trial (1988)

The Turn to Industry

Forging a proletarian party

JACK BARNES

Pathfinder
NEW YORK   LONDON   MONTREAL   SYDNEY

Edited by Steve Clark and Mary-Alice Waters

ISBN 978-1-60488-110-3
Library of Congress Control Number 2019949279
Manufactured in Canada

COVER DESIGN: Toni Gorton

COVER IMAGE: Patrick Heron (1920–1999), *Scarlet, Lemon and
Ultramarine: March 1957*, oil paint on canvas, 24 x 72 inches. © 2019
Artists Rights Society (ARS), New York / DACS, London / Tate,
London.

Pathfinder
www.pathfinderpress.com
E-mail: pathfinder@pathfinderpress.com

CONTENTS

PHOTO SECTIONS FOLLOW PAGES 24, 50, 64, AND 124

OTHER PHOTOS AND ILLUSTRATIONS

ABOUT THE AUTHOR

Jack Barnes is national secretary of the Socialist Workers Party. He joined the SWP in May 1961 and has been a member of the party's National Committee since 1963 and a national officer since 1968.

Barnes joined the Young Socialist Alliance in December 1960, soon after a trip to revolutionary Cuba in July and August that year. On his return, he helped organize at Carleton College in Minnesota one of the largest and most active campus chapters of the Fair Play for Cuba Committee. Since joining the SWP, he has been a leader of the party's defense of Cuba's socialist revolution.

While organizer of the SWP branch in Chicago and YSA Midwest organizer, Barnes was a central leader of the successful four-year campaign to defend three YSA members in Bloomington, Indiana, indicted in 1963 for "assembling" to advocate the overthrow of the State of Indiana by force and violence. In 1965 he was elected YSA national chairman and became director of the SWP and YSA's work to advance the growing movement against the Vietnam War. In January 1965 Barnes met twice with Malcolm X to conduct an interview published in the *Young Socialist* magazine.

Since the mid-1970s Barnes has led the political course of the SWP and its sister parties worldwide to build communist parties whose members and leaders in their large majority are workers and unionists organizing workers to forge and strengthen trade unions and lead the working class and its allies toward a successful socialist revolution.

Barnes is a contributing editor of *New International* magazine and author of numerous books and articles on revolutionary working-class politics and the communist movement. Titles include *Are They Rich Because They're Smart? Class, Privilege, and Learning Under Capitalism*; *The Clintons' Anti-Working-Class Record: Why Washington Fears Working People*; *Malcolm X, Black Liberation, and the Road to Workers Power*; *Cuba and the Coming American Revolution*; *Their Trotsky and Ours*; "US Imperialism Has Lost the Cold War"; and "The Stewardship of Nature Also Falls to the Working Class: In Defense of Land and Labor."

INTRODUCTION

Jack Barnes

The Turn to Industry: Forging a Proletarian Party is about the working-class program, composition, and course of conduct of the only kind of party worthy of the name "revolutionary" in the imperialist epoch. The only kind of party that can recognize the most revolutionary fact of this epoch—the worth of working people, and our power to change society when we organize and act against the capitalists and all the economic, social, and political forms of their class rule.

This book is about building such a party in the United States and in other capitalist countries around the world. It is about the course the Socialist Workers Party and its predecessors have followed for one hundred years and counting.

"We will not succeed in rooting the party in the working class, much less in defending the revolutionary proletarian principles of the party from being undermined, unless the party is an overwhelmingly proletarian party, composed in its decisive majority of workers in the factories, mines, and mills," emphasized resolutions adopted by the SWP convention in 1938. The party must become "an inseparable part of the trade unions and their struggles." It must be an inseparable part of daily battles waged by the working class and other exploited producers to defend ourselves and our families against the brutal consequences of capitalist oppression.

9

That orientation—the course of the Bolsheviks under V.I. Lenin in leading the workers and peasants to power in October 1917—has been our strategic course since a communist party was founded in the United States two years later, along with others affiliating to the new Communist International. The new party had one sole aim—emulating the Bolsheviks' example. The SWP is the direct descendant of that party.

With the rise of industrial capitalism some two hundred fifty years ago, conflicts between workers and employers increasingly took on "the character of collisions between two classes," explained Karl Marx and Frederick Engels in the Communist Manifesto, the founding program of the revolutionary workers movement. In face of the capitalists' cutthroat drive for profits, workers have no choice but to "club together in order to keep up the rate of wages" and resist employers' push to extend the workday and speed up production, with cold disregard for our health and safety. Inevitably, workers "begin to form combinations (trade unions)" against the employing class.

Some two centuries of class-struggle experience have confirmed that such "combinations" take many initial forms—from acts of resistance on the job; to battles against company lockouts; to strikes, organizing drives, and campaigns to expand union power.

The Turn to Industry: Forging a Proletarian Party is a new edition of the book first published in 1981 under the title *The Changing Face of US Politics: Working-Class Politics and the Trade Unions*. It is intended to be read, and above all used, as a guide to building a revolutionary workers party. Along with documents from earlier editions selected to focus on fundamental questions at the heart of the Socialist Workers Party's turn to industry from the 1970s on, it also includes three new pieces that give further concreteness to these reports.

Two of them are from the pages of the *Militant* news-weekly—one on the Steelworkers Fight Back campaign of the mid-1970s, the other a column by party veteran Marvel Scholl entitled "The Making of a Union Bureaucrat." The third is from a February 1980 report by Ken Shilman, who organized the work of party members in the United Mine Workers union at the time, drawing a balance sheet on the first two years of party building and trade union activity in the coalfields of West Virginia, Pennsylvania, and Alabama.

"We will not succeed in defending the party's revolutionary proletarian principles from being undermined unless the party is an overwhelmingly proletarian party in composition."

During the 1960s the SWP and its affiliated youth organization, the Young Socialist Alliance, had grown rapidly, recruiting large numbers of new members who had been won to the revolutionary working-class movement as students fighting Jim Crow segregation—North and South—as well as organizing against the Vietnam War and the oppression of women. In February 1978 the party's National Committee adopted the first report in this collection, "Leading the Party Into Industry," and began a historic turn.

Members of the party responded with enthusiasm, as well as disciplined attention to every detail. By the mid-1980s the large majority of party members were carrying out union and political work alongside other workers in auto plants, steel mills, rail yards, coal mines, oil refineries, electrical equipment factories, garment shops, textile mills, packinghouses, airports, and other industrial workplaces. Readers will find the breadth of this activity captured in the reports and the new and greatly expanded photo pages throughout the book.

Over the years since the SWP made what has become known as the turn to industry, the imperialist order has sunk into deeper and deeper crisis: declining profit rates; intensifying global capitalist competition; stagnation in capital investment to expand plant, equipment, and industrial employment; mounting pressures toward currency wars; and unending military conflicts. Workers and our families face attacks by the capitalist class, its government, and its Democratic and Republican parties, with their "socialist" wings, on our living and job conditions—on our very life and limb.

The rulers' blows don't fall evenly or with the same force on all sections of working people. Inequalities are widening not only between social classes but within the working class itself.

In face of these unrelenting assaults, the working class and labor movement have been in retreat since the 1990s, one symptom of which has been the sharp decline in union organization. Union membership in privately owned workplaces has fallen from more than 20 percent when the reports in this book were given to 6.5 percent today. The drop has been steep among industrial workers—from 87 percent of underground coal miners in 1977 to some 20 percent in 2018; from more than 90 percent of automobile workers in the late 1970s to some 50 percent today; with comparable trends among other mining and manufacturing workers.

But the necessity—and opportunities—for working

people, nonunion and union alike, to be bold, to organize ourselves, and to mobilize mutual solidarity have seldom been greater. And necessity is pushing us in that direction. The measure of our success will often not initially be the formation of new and powerful unions fighting for the interests of our class.

It will be the experience and confidence workers gain as we act together.

It will be our increasing political knowledge and consciousness of the employers—and of ourselves.

It will be our pride and our readiness to stand up and be counted as we act together as part of a common class.

And it will be our deeper understanding, explained by Engels as far back as 1847, that "communism is not a doctrine but a movement; it proceeds not from principles but from facts." It is the line of march of the working class toward political power.

> **"The rulers' blows don't fall evenly or with the same force on all sections of working people. Inequalities are widening not only between social classes but within the working class itself."**

Socialist Workers Party members today work and fight alongside rail workers—freight conductors to yard workers—confronting concession contracts, cuts in crew size, and increasingly dangerous job conditions as a result of the carriers' profit drive. We work and fight alongside workers at large retail stores owned by Walmart, the biggest private employer in the United States, with a nonunion workforce of some 1.5 million. We carry out political activity with car service and taxi drivers—from Africa, Asia, North America, and elsewhere who are working longer and longer hours under conditions of plunging take-home pay, unsustainable debt, and rising suicide rates in face of cutthroat competition among them fostered by owners of the fleet companies and "gig economy," "woke" capitalists.

The workers most open today to acting against the employers and to giving consideration to working-class political alternatives are those the capitalist families and the professional and upper middle classes dismiss as "deplorables" or smear as "criminals" or just "trash." Those contemptuous slurs are the opposite of the Socialist Workers Party's knowledge of the big majority of our class. We consider them a better class of people. We come from them. We're part of them.

These are men and women of all skin colors and ages. They and their kin come from urban and rural backgrounds, from all continents and national origins. It is among these "deplorables" that a disciplined and fighting union vanguard of the working class—and above all a tested class-conscious political vanguard, independent of the Democratic and Republican parties—will be forged and steeled over time in struggle against the employing class.

∼

The Turn to Industry: Forging a Proletarian Party stands on the revolutionary continuity of the Socialist Workers Party, explained and defended some eight decades ago in *In Defense of Marxism* by Leon Trotsky and *The Struggle for a Proletarian Party* by James P. Cannon. The articles and correspondence in those two books record the successful effort to maintain a communist course in face of an opposition in the party and its youth organization that began bending to imperialist pressure and public opinion during Washington's buildup to enter World War II. "The opposition is under the sway of petty-bourgeois moods and tendencies. This is the essence of the whole matter," Trotsky wrote in December 1939 in one of his articles collected in *In Defense of Marxism*. "Any serious factional fight in a party is always in the final analysis a reflection of the class struggle." That's why, as Trotsky explained in a letter written a few weeks later, "The class composition of the party must correspond to its class program."

Trotsky had become by early 1917 a central part of the Bolshevik leadership forged by Lenin that led the workers and peasants of Russia in making the October 1917 revolution and two years later launching the Communist International. In 1929, some half a decade after Lenin's death, Joseph Stalin banished Trotsky from the Soviet Union for leading the fight to continue Lenin's proletarian internationalist policies. Trotsky did so in direct political opposition to the rising petty bourgeois layers in the USSR whose privileges and interests were increasingly safeguarded by Stalin. Proletarian revolutionists the world over, including Cannon and other leaders of what became the Socialist Workers Party, joined with Trotsky in founding a new world communist movement loyal to Lenin's course.

The Turn to Industry: Forging a Proletarian Party also builds on Farrell Dobbs's firsthand account of the class-struggle leadership that organized and led workers across the Midwest in the 1930s in the strikes and union drives that transformed the Teamsters into a fighting industrial union movement. Dobbs's four books—*Teamster Rebellion, Teamster Power, Teamster Politics,* and *Teamster Bureaucracy*—"are worth reading, rereading, and reviewing every year," as I explain in one of the reports published here. "The more comrades get into industry, get to know the unions, and begin operating as part of party fractions, the more we'll get out of those books every time we go back to them."

It is also important to see *The Turn to Industry: Forging a Proletarian Party* as a companion to three other more recent works that expand on social and class issues at the heart of America's road to socialism:

• *Malcolm X, Black Liberation, and the Road to Workers Power* by Jack Barnes (2009);

• *Are They Rich Because They're Smart? Class, Privilege, and Learning Under Capitalism* by Jack Barnes (2016); and

• *Tribunes of the People and the Trade Unions* by Karl Marx, V.I. Lenin, Leon Trotsky, Farrell Dobbs, and Jack Barnes (2019).

> **"The workers most open to acting against the employers are those the capitalists and professional middle classes dismiss as 'deplorables,' 'criminals,' or just 'trash.' We consider them a better class of people. We come from them. We're part of them."**

Tribunes of the People and the Trade Unions centers on the party's broad and systematic propaganda activity in the working class. SWP members, supporters, and young socialists support picket lines, knock on doors, and stand on porches to talk with working people in cities, towns, and farm country, as we carry out such activity on the job and in the unions. We use the *Militant* newsweekly, books on working-class politics, and our SWP election campaigns to explain the truth about the capitalist parties and the exploitation, oppression, and wars by capital they uphold. *Above all, we report how working people are organizing to resist* assaults on our rights and conditions of life and work—on the job and off.

The *Militant* has tremendous leverage to advance the organization and education of class-struggle-minded workers and unionists. As a "newsweekly published in the interests of working people," which the *Militant's* masthead proudly proclaims, each issue features firsthand reports by working people—written in our own voices, and in our own names—about resistance to the capitalist rulers in factories, mines, and other workplaces and working-class communities. We do so openly and boldly as who we are and what we stand for, never pretending to be anything different. And we back our co-workers in acting the same way.

Tribunes of the People and the Trade Unions also features Trotsky's 1940 article, "Trade Unions in the Epoch of Imperialist Decay," which, as Farrell Dobbs wrote in a 1969 preface, contains "more food for thought (and action) . . . than will be found in any book by anyone else on the union question."

Malcolm X, Black Liberation, and the Road to Workers Power, as emphasized in its very first paragraphs, explains the unbreakable link between the fight for Black freedom and a course toward the "revolutionary conquest of state power by a politically class-conscious and organized vanguard of the working class—millions strong." A workers and farmers government, it says, is "the mightiest weapon possible" to wage the battle to end not only racism and Black oppression but also the subjugation of women "and every form of exploitation and human degradation inherited from millennia of class-divided society."

The introduction to that book explains why it is dedicated to SWP cadres who are African American, "who have never tired of getting in the face of race-baiters, red-baiters, and outright bigots and demagogues of every stripe who have sought to deny that workers, farmers, and young people who are Black—and *proud* to be Black—can and will become communists along the same road and on the same political basis as anyone else."

∼

There is a concerted attack today on the recognition that class divisions underlie *all* forms of exploitation and oppression, and that class struggle and class consciousness—*working-class consciousness*—are central to any effective fight for liberation. The assault comes not directly from the capitalist ruling families themselves, who have always tried to hide that dangerous truth—dangerous *to them*.

Instead, the offensive comes from what many refer to as "the left," liberals and radicals among the middle class and professionals—from privileged college and university campuses such as Harvard, Oberlin, and others; to prominent newspapers, magazines, and TV networks from the *New York Times* and *Atlantic Monthly* to CNN, BBC, and *The New Yorker*. It is promoted on websites and "social media" proliferating too rapidly to keep track of. These voices—which include individuals and political groups claiming to speak on behalf of working people and the oppressed—insist that conflicts based on race, skin color, or what they call "gender"—not class—are the driving force of history.

But the observation that the record "of all hitherto existing society is the history of class struggles" remains as true today as it was nearly 175 years ago when Karl Marx and Frederick Engels pointed it out at the opening of the Communist Manifesto, the founding program of the modern revolutionary workers movement.

Denial of the class struggle is nothing new. There are more than enough grandparents to current "theories" about "identity politics," "intersectionality," and so on noisily propagated by young professionals and other upper middle class layers today. In 1940 James P. Cannon polemicized against petty bourgeois currents on the eve of World War II who "rail at our stick-in-the-mud attitude toward the fundamental concepts of Marxism—the class theory of the state, the class criterion in the appraisal of all political questions, the conception of politics, including war, as the expression of class interests, and so forth and so on.

"There is a concerted attack today on the recognition that class divisions underlie all forms of oppression, and that class struggle and working-class consciousness are central to any fight for liberation."

"From all this," said Cannon, "they conclude that we are 'conservative' by nature, and extend that epithet to cover everything we have done in the past."

The epithet today is not simply "conservative," but some variant of "homophobe" or "racist," leveled against the working class by self-anointed "social justice warriors." Many of them resort to slander and thuggery to intimidate those they come into conflict with, whether over political differences, relations between the sexes, or small shopkeepers merely protecting themselves from shoplifting or other depredations. Showing disdain for due process and constitutional protections conquered in class battles by workers, African Americans, women, and others, these sanctimonious inquisitors organize to smear, shout down, and silence their chosen antagonists.

The real targets, however, are tens of millions of working people across the US, whom these scornful (and sometimes newly minted) bearers of class privilege seek to drum out of the human race as ignorant, backward, racist, and reactionary. But these "deplorables" are simply the current generations of workers whom the bosses—as well as many union officials—wrote off as "trash" during the great labor battles that exploded to their shock in the 1930s.

What I wrote in *Are They Rich Because They're Smart?* about today's self-designated "enlightened meritocracy" has been confirmed many times over. This "handsomely remunerated" layer—university presidents, deans, and professors; high-and-mighty officials of "nonprofits" and NGOs; media and hi-tech professionals; entertainment and sports personalities; and many others—"is determined to con the world into accepting the myth that the economic and social advancement of its members is just reward for their individual intelligence, education, and 'service.'" They truly believe they have "the right to make decisions, to administer and 'regulate' society for the bourgeoisie—on behalf of what they claim to be the interests of 'the people.'"

But above everything else, "they are mortified to be identified with working people in the United States— Caucasian, Black, or Latino; native- or foreign-born. Their attitudes toward those who produce society's wealth, the foundation of all culture, extend from saccharine condescension to occasional and unscripted open contempt, as they lecture us on our manners and mores."

A few years on, the only update needed is the allusion to their open contempt being "occasional" and "unscripted." Today it's both frequent and intentional.

∿

Working people have nothing to gain and everything to lose by relying on the propertied families, their capitalist two-party system, their "socialist" water carriers among professionals and the upper middle class, and their government and state. We must organize ourselves independently, both politically and organizationally, of the propertied classes who derive their enormous wealth and power from exploiting the social labor of workers, farmers, and other toiling producers—and who above all work to conceal that reality from us in order to retard the development of *class consciousness.*

"A socialist revolution is inconceivable without organizing our class to fight to build unions and union power. And forging a proletarian party, aimed at changing which class exercises state power, is impossible without joining in that struggle."

Today, the program and course of action presented in *The Turn to Industry: Forging a Proletarian Party* are needed by working people whether fighting for unpaid wages in a mine in Kentucky; organizing to resist unsafe working conditions in a massive retail conglomerate or on a two-hundred-car freight train; defending a woman's right to choose abortion; demanding amnesty for undocumented immigrants; mobilizing against cop brutality; or organizing solidarity with struggles by working people anywhere in the world.

Class-conscious workers openly and boldly join in every fight, every "combination" we can to resist the bosses' assaults, whether or not we've yet forged a union in our workplace.

We join in the pressing task of rebuilding and strengthening the labor movement, taking part in and championing efforts to organize the unorganized wherever workers are fighting, whatever the official status of their "papers."

And we explain the need for and help advance *class* consciousness, which *unites* not divides us, as we begin to transform ourselves and the trade unions into instruments of struggle against capitalist rule and exploitation itself.

There are no guarantees about what percentage of our class will become organized into unions, or how many unions will be transformed. "We're not prophets but revolutionaries who work to steer developments in the direction of strengthening the unity of the working class in struggle," notes the report in these pages that draws lessons the SWP learned from the first year of our turn to industry.

In the two great socialist revolutions of the twentieth century—in Russia in 1917, and then some four decades later in Cuba—the centrality of trade unions and the fight to transform them came largely after, not before, the struggle for workers power. But revolutionary-minded workers can't bank on that pattern being repeated in today's world, in which both the level of industrialization and the size and weight of the working class are much larger, not only in imperialist countries but also many others.

One thing we know for sure, however, is that a socialist revolution in the United States is inconceivable *without organizing our class to fight to build unions* and *to use union power* to advance the interests of working people here and around the world. And the forging of a proletarian party—a revolutionary *political* instrument of the working class, aimed above all at changing which class is exercising state power—is impossible without participating in that struggle.

"Malcolm X, Che Guevara and Fidel Castro, Maurice Bishop, Thomas Sankara. They never stopped reminding us that discovering our worth is more important than harping on our oppression. That we can transform ourselves as together we transform the foundations of society itself."

The biggest obstacle to class consciousness is what all the institutions of capitalist society teach working people to think of ourselves. What we're taught about our worth as human beings. What we're told we're *not* capable of doing and never will be. What we're lectured about day in and day out by the bosses and their middle class "experts" and "regulators," much of it echoed by union bureaucrats.

But the class struggle has a different story to tell. Malcolm X, Ernesto Che Guevara and Fidel Castro, Maurice Bishop, Thomas Sankara, and other outstanding revolutionary leaders never tired of reminding working people why discovering *our worth* is more important than harping on our oppression and exploitation. Of explaining what we *are* capable of becoming. And of showing us in action how we *are* capable of transforming ourselves—and the foundations of society itself—*as we organize together and fight.*

It is through such class battles, which include all social and political struggles in the interests of working people, that we gain experience and confidence, in ourselves and in each other. It's how ties of class solidarity and loyalty are forged. The SWP's program adopted in 1938, and still guiding our course today, tells the truth as well as it is possible to do:

"All methods are good that raise the class-consciousness of the workers, their trust in their own forces, their readiness for self-sacrifice in the struggle. The impermissible methods are those that implant fear and submissiveness in the oppressed in the face of their oppressors, that crush the spirit of protest and indignation or substitute for the will of the masses—the will of the leaders; for conviction—compulsion; for an analysis of reality—demagogy and frame-up."

There's nothing to add today to the closing sentences of that program. The Socialist Workers Party "uncompromisingly gives battle to all political groupings tied to the apron strings of the bourgeoisie. Its task—the abolition of capitalism's domination. Its aim—socialism. Its method—the proletarian revolution."

September 27, 2019

"As workers begin organizing together, the measure of our success often won't be the formation of new and powerful unions. It will be the experience and confidence we gain. It will be our consciousness, our readiness to stand up and be counted as part of a common class."

_____

"The necessity—and opportunities—for workers, nonunion and union alike, to be bold, organize ourselves,

SYDNEY BOLES

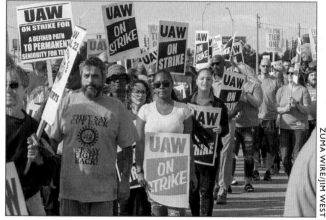

ZUMA WIRE/JIM WEST

Top: Harlan County, Kentucky, July 2019. Miners block rail tracks to prevent Blackjewel Coal Co. from hauling coal until bosses pay wages they are owed. After declaring bankruptcy earlier that month, company pulled final paychecks out of miners' bank accounts. The miners, who are not in a union, have won broad backing for their determined fight.

Bottom: Detroit, September 2019. Pickets at General Motors plant. Nearly 49,000 UAW members on strike at 55 factories and warehouses across US demand permanent status for temporary workers and the end of divisive two-tier pay scale.

and mobilize mutual solidarity have seldom been greater. And necessity is pushing us in that direction."

JOHN STEELE/MILITANT

UNITED ELECTRICAL WORKERS

Top: Lac-Mégantic, Quebec, October 2015. Rail workers, townspeople, and other supporters march for rail safety, two years after runaway oil train with one-person "crew" derailed, killing 47 and incinerating town center. Sign reads, "Never again!" Protesters blamed rail bosses and government, not engineer, for disaster.

Bottom: Erie, Pennsylvania, February 2019. Members of United Electrical Workers on strike at Wabtec locomotive plant, resisting company demand for two-tier wages for new hires and other steep concessions.

"In the battles against Black oppression, the subjugation of women, and every form of exploitation and

JAKE MYSLIWCZYK

JANET POST/MILITANT

Top: Pittsburgh, March 2019. High school and university students walk out of school to protest acquittal of cop who killed African American teenager Antwon Rose. As participants in these actions, socialist workers explain that the problems the oppressed and exploited face are products of the capitalist system.

Bottom: Bridgeton, New Jersey, March 2019. Workers rally to demand driver's licenses for undocumented immigrants. Lea Sherman, Socialist Workers Party candidate for New Jersey state assembly, addressed demonstrators, calling on labor movement to fight for amnesty for all immigrants.

human degradation, the mightiest weapon possible is a workers and farmers government."

Top: St. Paul Minnesota, May 2019. Action in defense of a woman's right to choose abortion, one of hundreds protesting sharp restrictions on access to abortion by several state legislatures, including Alabama law criminalizing nearly all abortions.

Bottom: Jacksonville, Florida, October 2018. Marchers demand voting rights for former prisoners. A few weeks later a big majority in Florida approved a ballot initiative to restore that right to more than a million working people who had been disenfranchised.

"**Working people must organize independent** of the capitalist class, its two-party system, and its government. We must break politically from the class whose wealth and power derive from exploiting our labor—and who work to conceal that reality from us in order to retard the development of class consciousness."

Leading the party into industry

In 1978 the Socialist Workers Party's National Committee voted to lead the party in carrying out what became known as "the turn to industry." The report below, which initiated that turn, was adopted by the SWP National Committee on February 24, 1978. It was published for all members in the party's internal *Discussion Bulletin* and debated and voted on in every party branch. The report was adopted by delegates to the August 1979 SWP national convention.

This meeting of the National Committee has one overriding goal. The Socialist Workers Party must subordinate everything else to immediately organize to get the great majority of our membership into industry and the industrial trade unions. We must do this in such a way that the majority of members of branch executive committees, of local executive committees, and of the National Committee, the party's highest leadership body between conventions, will soon be made up of comrades who are active members of industrial unions.

This party effort must be a universal one. It will be carried out by *every* branch and local.[1] There are no exceptional cities in this country where we have branches but where no surplus value is produced by industrial workers.

The turn is also universal in the sense that it relates to *every* member of the party, employed and unemployed, new and experienced. Every comrade without exception should now sit down with the branch leadership and review their job, their assignments, the city they live in, their various contributions—and decide how they will join in the turn's implementation.

This is not another "area of work." This is not a "campaign" of the party. This is not "one of the important tasks" of the party or "one of our main axes of work." This is not counterposed to other things we're doing. This is the underpinning of the party's political activity in the immediate future—without qualification, and beginning *now*.

It is together with *workers in industry* that we want to carry out all campaigns. This is where we intend to take the *Militant* and Socialist Workers Party election campaigns and introduce all our activities. This is who we want to influence and recruit to the party. *This is the power we fight to mobilize on behalf of the resistance by the exploited and oppressed, all over the world.*

This is where the majority of the future leaders of successful battles for women's liberation and of the struggles of the African American population as well as other oppressed nationalities will come from. This will become the central arena for the development, training, and testing of our cadres.

It is workers in industry who are our milieu and our

---

1. See glossary: Socialist Workers Party branches, locals, districts.

central audience. Their potentially powerful unions are our base.

What we propose is a *political* move for the party. Not a hygienic or therapeutic one. We are not doing this to cleanse the party of petty-bourgeois elements. But we can't end with that statement, either. Because the class composition of the party does pose a challenge. We will not become a party whose big majority are industrial workers automatically. It must be organized. It must be consciously *led*.

The big changes facing the capitalist class on a world scale make this political move not only necessary but timely. It flows from the need of the American ruling class to drive forward their offensive, and to make industrial workers and their unions more and more the target. Above all, our judgment flows from changes in the attitudes of the working class *in response* to this offensive.

We are in a preparatory period—not a period when we are leading mass class-struggle actions. We must make no mistake about that. But it is a preparatory period in which the *center of American politics has shifted to the industrial working class.* That's the central political judgment we put before the National Committee.

If we did not bring about a significant and rapid change in the composition of the party, we would place ourselves, *now unnecessarily,* outside the arena in which the decisive changes and developments are happening in the class struggle. We would not have our hand on the pulse of the working class, feeling the real rhythm of its developments and changes. We would cut ourselves off from the center of American politics.

By making this move quickly, we will get rid of any disorientation in priorities and perspectives that comes from the party not *living* in the center of the most important political developments that are occurring. When new comrades join the SWP, or when Young Socialist Alliance members who are on campus graduate to party membership, it will be automatic for them to consult the party leadership to help make a decision as to which city they move to and what industry they work in.

The only way to accomplish this turn is by consciously acting—and doing it *now*. Guiding the political implementation of this decision is the central task of the party leadership at every level, from the branch executive committees to the Political Committee.[2]

To accelerate the proletarianization of the party by changing the jobs of the majority of the SWP members is, of course, a *tactical* question. It's not the same thing as the Socialist Workers Party's historic proletarian orientation. That course was born in 1903 with the emergence of the organized Bolshevik current within the Russian Social Democratic Labor Party under Lenin's leadership. In the United States it began in 1919 with the founding of the Communist Party as the section here of the newly formed Communist International. To this day, that has been the continuity of the Socialist Workers Party.

Adopting this tactic of sending the majority of comrades into industry, and doing it today, however, is a historic decision in many ways. It affects everything we do.

If we fail to do this, the party will regress, it will slide back on its accomplishments and miss opportunities. We will become disoriented and begin making unnecessary political errors. And this will include defaulting in our responsibility to set an example for our entire world movement.[3]

---

2. See glossary, Socialist Workers Party National Committee.

3. "The Turn and Building a World Communist Movement," a report by Jack Barnes discussed and adopted by the 1979 World Congress of the Fourth International, appears on p. 151 of this book.

For worker-bolsheviks, trade union work, properly understood, means finding ways to advance the development of a mass leadership, a working-class vanguard, that thinks socially and acts politically. It means providing class-conscious leadership for struggles of the oppressed. It means carving out a class-struggle left wing in the labor movement, and advancing the fight for independent working-class political action—a clear class break from the Democratic, Republican, and other bourgeois and petty-bourgeois parties. Carried out in this way, trade union work, that is, organizing workers, now becomes the central political responsibility of every single leading committee.

We're at a new stage in the party's history, a new stage in the development of its leadership. This is a test, but above all it is a historic opportunity. Members of the party are waiting for the leadership to lead on this proletarian turn, and there's every reason to think they will respond.

We're not seeking immediate conjunctural gains. We're not doing this because of the coal miners strike that began in December and is still holding strong,[4] or because we're excited over some contacts we've made somewhere.

We are doing this because this turn is the only concrete way right now to implement and carry forward the basic proletarian orientation the party has had since its founding in 1919. It's the only way to deepen the work we began in 1975 as we saw new political openings in the working class and unions. It's the only tactic now available to us that advances and does not cut across our communist strategy.

Six basic questions
The purpose of this report is to present the basic orientation we have and the leadership conclusions we draw if we

---

4. See glossary: Coal strike (1977–78).

adopt this proposal by the Political Committee. The best way to do this is to pose a series of basic questions.

First: Why now? I've already said why postponing such a move would undermine the party's historic proletarian orientation. But why didn't we make this decision earlier?

Second: Why industry, with special attention to basic industry? Why concentrate on industrial unions rather than on the American Federation of State, County, and Municipal Employees (AFSCME), the Office and Professional Employees International Union (OPEIU), the American Federation of Teachers (AFT), the National Education Association (NEA), or some other unions?

Third: What is the concrete character of the ruling-class offensive against workers in industry? What political line best counters this offensive? And how does this affect the movements and needs of the allies of labor?

Fourth: What is communist trade union work in industry? What does the party miss by not having the overwhelming majority of its members there?

Fifth: What is a worker-bolshevik? What are the structural and organizational implications of becoming a party of worker-bolsheviks?

Sixth: What must be the character of the leadership of this kind of party? What new light can we shed on this in view of the progress we have made the last year on what James P. Cannon called the question of questions—the conscious development of the leadership of the revolutionary party?

Why now?

Why now? Why not earlier?

Part of this is relatively easy to answer. We did not make this move before the 1974–75 recession, which was a turning point for capitalism not just in the United States but worldwide. That downturn was the first since the end of World War II to shake the major capitalist countries simultaneously.

To have made the move we're now deciding prior to such a shift in the postwar capitalist world would have been a gamble. It could easily have turned into a gimmick. It would have disoriented the party. It would not have been tied to real developments in world capitalism and in the working class and political life in the US.

Prior to 1974 much of the political activity in this country took a course around, and not through, either the industrial unions or workers in industry. But following Nixon's 1971 wage-price freeze, and as we got closer to the 1974–75 worldwide downturn, the course of a previous entire period began to change.[5]

We don't base the party's course on conjunctural economic estimates, and we predict no Armageddon. But we know that by the mid-1970s we had entered a period of crisis for world capitalism—one we will not come out of without gigantic battles for power. That's what we are convinced of.

What's more, this imperialist economic and social crisis was accompanied by important developments in world politics. In 1974 the fall of the exhausted fascist dictatorship in Portugal unleashed big struggles by workers and working farmers there. It accelerated national liberation struggles in Lisbon's African colonies and led to the independence of Mozambique, Cape Verde, Guinea-Bissau, and Angola. That same year, the monarchy in Ethiopia was overturned, opening deep-going struggles for land reform and other antifeudal measures in that large East African nation.

---

5. See glossary: Recession (1974–75); and Wage-price freeze (1971).

In 1975 Vietnamese liberation fighters marched into Saigon—now Ho Chi Minh City—as the last remaining US forces fled in a massive helicopter airlift. Those events culminated a decades-long battle for national freedom and reunification, first against French and then US imperialism. "Vietnam: Victory for All Oppressed" was the *Militant*'s front-page banner headline that week.

Later that year Cuban volunteer combatants, responding to a call for international solidarity from the newly independent government in Angola, launched a military campaign to repel invading troops of South Africa's white supremacist regime. By early 1976 the last South African troops had been pushed out; that setback for the racist regime helped inspire a mass uprising in Soweto of youth and working people that same year, as well as the rise of a worldwide campaign to bring down apartheid.

That's the first part of the answer to the question: Why not earlier?

But then there's another part.

Why not 1974–75 instead of 1978?

First, we had to absorb not only the character of the worldwide recession but the conjunctural recovery that would inevitably follow. The initial years of the so-called upturn in the US have seen more jobs but also high levels of both inflation and unemployment, as well as an escalation in the ruling-class offensive against workers on all fronts. We've had to absorb the effects of this offensive on the working class and the unions, and its concrete effect on the most oppressed sectors of the working class—African Americans, youth, women.

Second, we had to go through some experiences in the American labor movement. We had to go through the rise of Steelworkers Fight Back and see the real political and organizational possibilities, as well as the limits, of this stage of the changes among industrial workers.[6]

We responded with active solidarity to the strike on the Iron Range in Minnesota, where we saw every one of our assessments concerning the meaning of Steelworkers Fight Back verified. We've been part of rail workers' resistance to the carriers' offensive, including local experiences on the railroad in Chicago, Philadelphia, and elsewhere. We've had a variety of local experiences in the San Francisco Bay Area, Houston, Pittsburgh, and other places where we could probe, test, feel the changes and possibilities.

And now we're standing shoulder to shoulder with mine workers in the current showdown between the UMWA and the coal bosses and their government.[7] We're part of the ongoing fight by miners since the late 1960s that pushed back the scourge of black lung disease and won community health clinics in mining towns across Appalachia; that won union safety committees with the power to shut down production over health and safety issues; and that through the Miners for Democracy movement in the UMWA enabled its members to vote on their contracts and wield union power more effectively to defend the ranks.[8]

These experiences were necessary to know concretely what was changing and how much it was changing.

We had to go through the experience of seeing what it means to have more Blacks, more Chicanos, more Puerto Ricans, more women, more Vietnam veterans, and more

---

6. See "Steelworkers Fight To Take Back Their Union," the next item in this book, as well as glossary: Steelworkers Fight Back.

7. See glossary: Iron Range strike (1977); Milwaukee Road and freight carriers' offensive; Right to Vote Committee (UTU); Coal strike (1977–78).

8. See glossary: Miners for Democracy.

young workers in industry and the unions. We had to see in real life how the attitudes and reactions, the combativity—which we talked about and anticipated—began to manifest themselves.

We were able to see the importance of generational shifts in the composition of the working class, as literally hundreds of thousands of young workers came forward and got involved in this or that struggle. The majority were young, Caucasian, male workers. We saw many of them become open in a new way to what Socialist Workers Party members say about the capitalist crisis and about different sections of our proletarian program.

We saw them begin to express the changing attitudes we knew were coming, and thus understood better the differential effect of the rulers' offensive along generational lines as well as nationality, sex, and skill. We were able to confirm that we are not going to see the development of some sort of vanguard that's marked by being "nonwhite" or "nonmale."

We began seeing the dynamic between "bread-and-butter" issues and the broad social and political questions labor must face up to. We began to see a response—uneven, but broad—to political and social questions and campaigns brought into the labor movement. And we saw the links between this new response and the upswing in class combativity.

So these are the first two answers to "Why now?" One is the reality of the 1974–75 worldwide downturn, the subsequent recovery, and developments in world politics. And then the changes in the industrial working class in the United States, including changes in attitudes and consciousness.

But we had to go through something else before the decision we're making today. And maybe that third thing is the most important. Before we could make this move, the party had to have our *own* experiences and accomplishments within the labor movement. We had to get our feet wet in industry. The branches and locals, the union fractions, had to gain experience in industry. And that's what we've been doing since the mid-1970s.

For the first time in almost thirty years, we've had functioning and growing national industrial union fractions. We've had to learn how to lead this work at every level. We've had to learn to assess the possibilities as well as the frustrations and difficulties as we participated in developments such as Steelworkers Fight Back and the post–Steelworkers Fight Back period. We've had to learn how to use the *Militant,* our books, our political campaigns, our weekly forums and other party institutions.

In other words, we've had to enter a whole new stage in leadership understanding, experience, and political breadth. We've had to start by having leaders of the party on every level go into industry ourselves to lead this. We've had to see with our own eyes, in branch after branch, the impact this process was having on the individual comrades who took the lead by going into industry. It raised their spirits and gave them a political outlook, a new focus. Then we were ready to responsibly generalize.

That's why now, not earlier.

Why concentrate on industry?

Why concentrate on industry? Maybe this is sort of an embarrassing or unnecessary question for Marxists, since this is a cornerstone of Marxism, of communism. But it's worth reviewing both the economics and the politics.

The economics are simple. Raw materials like coal and ores and oil, and products like machine tools, steel, and major electrical components, have tremendous leverage in the economy. They enter into production in the earliest stages to make every single part of the economy run. Workers in industries producing raw materials and semi-finished products, or engaged in freight transportation, construction, and agriculture, have leverage because without them capitalist production and trade stop.

Capital goods—electrical equipment, automotive equipment, heavy manufacturing of all sorts—are simply different stages of the employing class purchasing and harnessing labor power to produce the gigantic wealth American workers create. At each stage, as you get farther from the "final" product, there's more strength, more leverage—from simply an economic point of view.

There's another economic side to this too. The labor expended by workers in these industries, their social labor—productive labor, as Marx described it—is the main source of surplus value. It is the major source of all those revenues used by the rulers not only to maintain and expand capitalist production, but to keep the government, service, and "professional" sectors of the economy going. By looking at it this way, we begin to see something that's not often talked about: the increasing, not decreasing, vulnerability of the modern capitalist economy.

The more complicated and highly organized the economy gets, the more vulnerable it becomes to stoppages, to disruptions in basic industry. This reality would come through even more clearly in the miners strike right now if the United Mine Workers had the entire coal industry organized, not only the heavily unionized Appalachia from Pennsylvania and West Virginia across to Alabama, Kentucky, Indiana, and Illinois, but also the largely unorganized Western coalfields.

The political side is even more important. From the point of view of the ruling capitalist families themselves, the class enemy, it doesn't take much to understand politically that coal is more important to them than social work. Their system can operate much easier and for longer periods without social workers than without coal. The capitalists don't even need social workers personally, since the rulers get *their* generous welfare checks straight from the trust departments of banks.

This becomes even clearer if you look at it from the standpoint of the competitive needs of US imperialism on a world scale. This social labor of workers in the United States is the source of the international power of American capitalism, the source of the rulers' exports of goods and capital.

These are the reasons that industrial workers, who are a minority of the American working class, have such fundamental strength, such potential power. This also demonstrates the empty fakery of the academic theories about the "new working class" and "postindustrial society."

But we must also look at the political side of this question from the point of view of *our* class, the working class.

First, much of industry is organized. This sounds obvious, but it has only been true for the past few decades in American history. Before the mid-1930s (in many ways before World War II), this was not true; basic industry was *not* organized. A relatively thin aristocracy of labor was organized, mainly in the skilled crafts. But now, to a significant degree, the mass of industrial workers are organized.[9]

---

9. Four decades later, in 2019, these gains have been eroded by the cumulative consequences of the union officialdom's class-collaborationist course described in these pages. In 1978, when this report was given, more than 20 percent of private-sector workers were union members; today that figure has fallen to 6.5 percent, comparable to levels that existed in the early 1930s before the organizing drives and working-class social movement that built the industrial unions. The steepest declines

Secondly, we need to consider the character of the industrial workplace and what the factory does socially and psychologically to workers. The social character of the work, the large concentration of workers, the extremely high division of labor—these factors give workers an awareness of our power, as well as the reality that this power can be exerted only when *collectively* harnessed and led.

The fact that collective bargaining—rather than individual relations with the bosses—governs so much of what is done leads to greater self-confidence among workers. It encourages "no contract–no work" consciousness even in periods of ruling-class offensive. As one miner recently explained on the TV news, when you're a baby, before you learn to say "mama" or "dada," you learn to say "no contract, no work."

It's important, third, to remember the changing age of the workforce in industry. There are many more younger workers, the so-called post-Vietnam generation the bosses keep complaining about in relation to the miners strike. And we've detailed the racial composition of selected industries many times in the last few years.

Fourth, we should note the radicalizing tradition of struggle in the industrial working class. It shouldn't be exaggerated, but it's real. The industrial unions were built in the massive struggles of the CIO. It took bloody battles to build the Auto Workers, to build the Teamsters in large regions of the country, to build the Steelworkers,

---

have been in unions representing workers in basic industries such as coal mining (87 percent of underground miners in 1977, some 20 percent in 2018) and auto assembly (more than 90 percent in the late 1970s, some 50 percent today). There have been comparable declines in unionization of workers in steel mills, workers represented by the International Association of Machinists, garment and textile, construction, and other basic industries.

"As one coal miner explained on the TV news, when you're a baby, before you learn to say 'mama' or 'dada,' you learn to say, 'No contract, no work.'"

UMWA

Above: Miners on strike against Blue Diamond Coal for union recognition Stearns, Kentucky, 1978.

NANCY COLE/MILITANT

Inset: Washington, DC, March 1978. Miners defied Carter administration's efforts to break 110-day nationwide UMWA strike through a back-to-work order.

etc. That tradition, even if much of the continuity is lost, still exists.

The fifth point is the degree to which many of these industrial unions affect much more than the industry, the factory, and the workforce itself. They affect large parts of the country. Take the current miners strike once again. When you talk about the stakes in the UMWA strike, you're talking about the health and welfare and future of all of Appalachia, an entire region of this country.

When you talk about the UAW, you're talking about the future of entire cities—Detroit for example.

Finally, and most important, the unionized industrial working class is where the brunt of the ruling class's attack more and more comes down. The rulers can beat down AFSCME members in state and local governments in different places. They can impose cutbacks on teachers. They can do all kinds of things like that, but it just begins the process. They must "tame" the industrial working class. They must "tame" the most strategically located producers. This is the target of the ruling-class offensive. That's why we put our priorities here.

We must maintain our central priority in steel and add rail and auto to our *national* priorities. In addition, we've got to take a look at local situations. In some places we'll put priority on the Machinists union, which has organized whole sectors of industry. Or the Oil, Chemical and Atomic Workers. Or the electrical industry and unions, or the shipyards, mining, transport—whatever fits into our national needs and makes sense in local areas.

As Jim Cannon said thirty-seven years ago, "We are a small party and we can't go colonizing all over the lot. We must colonize in those places which offer the best opportunity at the time, and when this opportunity which we seize at one occasion proves later on to be not so fruitful, we have got to shift our people."[10] It's a lot better to have a couple of viable and functioning *fractions* in a local or branch than to have a lot of "fractions" of one or two individual comrades each. That's a standard guide.

We need to set these priorities now and consciously say that we're "de-AFSCME-izing" the party. We are not doing so from the standpoint of downgrading the work we do in unions such as AFSCME or recruiting to the party any contacts we may have there. We're doing so from the point of view of where the party is going to assign people. We are not neutral or indifferent whether a comrade becomes a teacher, a social worker, gets into the OPEIU—or goes into industry. We want to help comrades get into industry and the industrial unions.

This doesn't mean we won't do work in, or pay careful attention to, AFSCME or the teachers unions.[11] The turn to industry will strengthen our work in the unions and labor movement as a whole. It does not detract from the importance of political struggles among teachers, for instance. In fact, as the party and our industrial union fractions grow, at some point we will decide to recruit fractions in unions of teachers, government employees, and so on.

But we must make a decision about what unions we are going to send comrades into, including party members who today are in AFSCME, the AFT, or the NEA. This

---

10. James P. Cannon, *The Socialist Workers Party in World War II* (Pathfinder, 1975), October 11, 1941 speech, p. 236 [2019 printing].

11. See glossary: AFSCME; AFT; NEA; OPEIU.

must be a conscious, explicit orientation of the party, with no ambiguities or exceptions.

Offensive against industrial workers

The third question is: What is the character of the current offensive against the industrial working class? What political response is needed?

I won't repeat what we've talked about before—the attacks today on public employees and social services; the differential impact of the offensive on oppressed nationalities, women, and youth; the rightward shift in bourgeois politics, which gives encouragement to the right amid increasing class polarization.

Here I want to focus on the particular character of the attacks on the industrial workers, on the industrial trade unions.

When we talk about the social and political responsibilities of labor, we explain the need to combat the ruling-class policy of imposing on *the individual family* the *entire* responsibility for social services that should be taken care of by society—the care of the young, the elderly, the sick and disabled.

But that's not the only way capitalism works. The employers also try to impose on *the individual worker* responsibilities that should be met by society. And more and more they try to establish that these responsibilities will be met only according to the profitability of each worker's own boss. I leave aside the most grotesque single examples, such as the public employee unions' officials sinking massive amounts of pension funds into city bonds in New York City. But more and more often, so-called fringe benefits—pensions, health-care plans, supplemental unemployment benefits—all become contingent on the continuing profits of the boss you work for. We see this growing in industries like coal, steel, and auto.

These benefits are not won for the class as a whole, or even a section of the class. These fringes are good in good times—*for workers who have them*—because they're a substantial addition to everything else industrial workers can count on. But when the squeeze comes, this all begins to fall apart. Your pension funds are threatened. Your healthcare plans are dismantled. The supplemental unemployment benefits run out. And the squeeze is on.

This is the payoff, this is where the debt of business unionism comes due.

This is the price paid for the class-collaborationist policy of refusing to fight for the real needs *of the working class.* The refusal to fight for the social security of the class, universal health care and unemployment benefits that are real and high enough to live on, for protection against inflation, and, above all, for a shorter workweek with no cut in pay.

And never forget, this is the price paid for a bureaucracy that rejects a course of independent working-class political action. The price paid for a labor officialdom that says social and political struggles are unnecessary; that the employers' promises in the contract can be counted on; that wings of the two imperialist parties are *our* political instrument.

This is the payoff for the refusal of the labor bureaucracy to fight for the broad social needs of the working class and to build a political instrument to fight for them. This concretizes the need for an independent labor party in a new and more understandable way, because now these problems are immediately facing the section of the working class—unionized workers in basic industry—that thought they were the least vulnerable and had the best deal.

The bosses' offensive is a conscious attack on trade union democracy. The *right to strike* also becomes a special target of the employers. Other red tape gets institutionalized as

"Class collaboration isn't simply an attitude of union bureaucrats. It takes the form of institutions that tie workers hand and foot, making them dependent on something other than their own power as a class."

As part of red tape, workers usually see only "contract summaries" supplied by officials; today's book-length pacts are impossible to read. Class-struggle leadership of Minneapolis Teamsters insisted that contracts be short and clear, often one page. There was no such thing as a no-strike clause. Here, pact with city's printing bosses, published in full in union's weekly newspaper, February 18, 1937.

well, such as lengthy probationary periods that give the bosses a chance to weed out union militants, "trouble-makers," the "walking wounded" of all kinds. Speedup and the erosion of safety and health protection on the job are more and more widespread.

Incentive pay and piecework are increasingly intro-duced in one form or another. Schemes like the Experi-mental Negotiating Agreement[12] in steel with its no-strike pledge are generalized by the employers. And arbitration procedures are put into every nook and cranny of every contract, tying workers' hands and leaving them without the right to use their strength to fight back. In this way class collaboration becomes institutionalized.

Class collaboration isn't simply an attitude of bureau-crats. Class collaboration takes the form of institutions that tie the individual worker hand and foot, that make a worker dependent on something other than the power of his or her co-workers and class. Trade union democracy of any kind, union control of conditions and pace of work, individual workers' rights on the job, are eroded more and more by concessions to the employers' offensive. The right to know what's in your contract, the right to vote on it, the right to elect your stewards and officers—these things can less and less be afforded by the employers. And they are less and less tolerated by the union bureaucracy as a result.

Finally, of course, class collaboration is sealed by total political dependence on the capitalists' parties and their governments.

The rulers' offensive has created a growing need for *sol-idarity*. Solidarity has become crucial to success in the struggles that are now breaking out. Each of these fights, like the one on the Iron Range, like that of the coal min-

---

12. See glossary: Experimental Negotiating Agreement.

ers today, turns into a political battle for the minds of the working class. Not only of the workers who are on strike but of the entire class. The strikers appeal for support, and the employers, the government, try to prevent that support—try to whip up opposition and division.

This is not only why solidarity is needed. It's also why we need internationalism. Because ultimately class solidarity has to be worldwide. It has to take on ruling-class policies such as protectionism, deportation of undocumented workers, chauvinistic "Buy American" campaigns, and so on.

What's more, to have real solidarity you must have it inside the union itself, within the working class itself. The elementary and immediate need for class solidarity—with the striking miners, with any strike—puts the spotlight on the importance of bringing the weight and power of the unions into the fight for Black rights, women's rights, and affirmative action. Without fighting for these rights, solidarity within the union and within the workforce itself is crippled.

Without programs like child care, without the needs of women being met and fought for, the fight for union democracy is weakened. Sections of the workforce are prevented from participating on an equal footing. The total workforce cannot be mobilized to make and carry out the decisions needed to struggle.

The employers' offensive has different effects on different layers of the working class. It hits hardest those who are least prepared to defend themselves. This fact poses directly and immediately the necessity for the labor movement to lead the fight for broad social needs of the unemployed, women, oppressed nationalities, immigrant workers, youth, working farmers, small truckers and fishermen operating their own vehicles or boats.

If the unions don't lead, they will reap a whirlwind of deepening suspicion and hatred by those who should be allies and even members. And that will ultimately be decisive.

This means that *Militant* articles must be written with more than just the workers most immediately affected in mind, but for the entire working class. It becomes more possible, and more necessary, to explain the *class* side of all questions.

To fight around these social issues, to fight the political battles, workers need a *labor party*—a party based on our most elementary class institutions, the trade unions. We need a political instrument that will advance the needs of the entire working class. This goes hand in hand with solidarity and trade union democracy.

We should argue the labor party question on all levels. Why do the capitalist politicians act the way they do? Including those who call themselves progressive, or left wing, or—yes—socialist? Why do they *have* to act that way? What are the connections between the capitalist parties and politicians and the employers, the cops, the government, the state? What are the concrete costs, in each case, to the whole working class of having no labor party fighting for the interests of workers and other exploited working people—the price paid for being unarmed in the political arena?

All this becomes easier, not harder, to explain effectively.

Parallel to all this, the union bureaucracy has less and less breathing space, less room to maneuver. They're trying to negotiate a contract to satisfy the boss. But if they don't negotiate a contract that's good enough for the ranks, at a certain stage workers won't want to have anything to do with them anymore.

Finally, something else becomes clear: the state of the

bureaucracy is not identical to the state of the unions. That's a big lesson from the strike on the Iron Range and from the coal miners strike. The union and the bureaucracy are different things. In fact, the union is weakened and crippled by the bureaucracy. And while the bureaucracy is more and more in a bind, under pressure, the rank and file of the unions is becoming more ready to fight, and more ready to think about new methods of struggle, new perspectives and programs.

What is trade union work?
What is trade union work in industry? That is our fourth question.

Properly understood, the simplest way to describe it is talking socialism with workers, that is, *organizing* workers. It's taking initiatives *together with* other workers, including to organize unions. It's strengthening class consciousness further, and maximizing workers' capacity and willingness to use union power against the bosses and their government. That's what trade union work is.

We do this working together, not simply as individuals. We do it through organized fractions, not scattershot, with each comrade on their own. This work is led by the party.

We're explaining the party's proletarian program, and putting it to work to guide our activity in the working class and the unions. We're selling subscriptions to the newspaper that advances the organization of the working class, as well as books and pamphlets by leaders of the party and revolutionary struggles. We're using our weekly forum series, SWP election campaigns, and other party institutions.

Our goal is to help workers, including party members, to become more confident in ourselves. To become more confident, *as we organize ourselves*, in our power and in our abilities. In the process, solidarity is strengthened at every turn.

There is no handbook that will make any comrade an overnight expert. Only class-struggle experience can mold that. There is one thing every comrade should read or re-read when they go into industry, however. It should be a kind of party law. That's Farrell Dobbs's four-book series on the Teamsters—*Teamster Rebellion, Teamster Power, Teamster Politics, Teamster Bureaucracy.*[13] It is unlikely a better "handbook" explaining all sides of Bolshevik trade union work can be found. [And a little more than four decades after this report was given, I would make two additions to that must-read list: Leon Trotsky's unfinished 1940 article "Trade Unions in the Epoch of Imperialist Decay," including Farrell's preface to a 1969 pamphlet featuring that article; and *Malcolm X, Black Liberation, and the Road to Workers Power,* published in 2009.[14]—JB]

There are no prescriptions we can distribute on how to do trade union work. But there are some things to keep in mind.

One is the variation that sometimes exists between the kind of work it's possible to do on the job and the kind you can do in the union. Sometimes you can do one and not the other, and then this can change rapidly and you can do both.

Second, we should take every opportunity to concretely talk about trade union democracy, independent labor political action, solidarity. Raise these questions, talk about

---

13. See glossary: Teamster series.

14. Trotsky's article had not been completed at the time of his assassination in August 1940. It, along with Dobbs's preface, can be found in *Tribunes of the People and the Trade Unions* by Karl Marx, V.I. Lenin, Leon Trotsky, Farrell Dobbs, and Jack Barnes (Pathfinder, 2019). *Malcolm X, Black Liberation, and the Road to Workers Power* by Barnes is also published by Pathfinder.

them, whenever we get an opportunity. There are a lot of variations here, too.

For instance, comrades at Bethlehem Steel's huge Sparrows Point mill in Baltimore report all kinds of discussions among steelworkers about the coal miners strike, how to support the miners, the importance of it. Black and Latino workers are taking the lead in explaining the need for solidarity and organizing accordingly.

But comrades in the Brooklyn shipyards, where union consciousness is lower, find they have to start by explaining why workers should be interested in the miners, why the miners struggle is significant. Especially some Black, Puerto Rican, Latino workers there say, "If they're making seven to eight dollars an hour [that would be $27–$31 an hour in 2019] with all those benefits, why should we be interested in giving them support?" It varies tremendously.

A third thing is to learn the industry, learn the skills, learn the unions, and help others to do so.

The fourth thing is to always see everything as a *fraction* effort. Never put a comrade in industry in a situation where he or she feels solely responsible, as an individual, for trade union work. Never ask them to give you a list of individual accomplishments. We don't do anything else that way. We don't individually credit one person for the results of an election campaign. We don't individually praise Fred Halstead because he was a leader of our work in the anti–Vietnam War movement when half a million people marched on Washington against the war.

Each comrade, of course, is individually responsible for what they do or don't do to carry out the party's trade union work along the lines the party has discussed and decided. But our political yardstick is what we accomplish together—in fractions, led by the party, alongside other

"Workers in industries producing or transporting raw materials and semifinished goods have leverage. Without them, capitalist production and trade stop."

Top: Strikers picket Tenneco shipyard in Newport News, Virginia, February 1979. Successful battle for recognition of Steelworkers Local 8888 registered strengthening of working class and unions as a result of Black rights victories in the South.

Bottom: Workers from Bethlehem Steel's Sparrows Point plant in Baltimore organized two busloads of union members to back strike at March 1979 rally of 3,500 in Newport News. SWP members were among the workers in the plant who built action.

"The 1974–75 global recession was a turning point for capitalism. It coincided with big developments in world politics—in Vietnam, Angola, southern Africa, Grenada, Nicaragua, and Iran."

VERDE OLIVO

THE MILITANT

Vietnam rebel gains: a victory for all humanity

Boston school plan: retreat on desegregation

Chicago: Daley's cops exposed as spies, burglars

Unions mobilize for April 26 March for Jobs

Memos bare FBI plot to sabotage SWP campaigns

New stage in Portuguese revolution

Top: When Angola declared independence in 1975, troops from South Africa invaded. In 16-year war, the army of the apartheid regime was defeated by Angolan troops and volunteers from Cuba. *Above,* August 1983, Angolan and Cuban forces celebrate victory after a key battle at Cangamba.

Bottom left: In April 1975 Vietnamese liberation fighters marched into Saigon—now Ho Chi Minh City—as the last remaining US forces fled.

Bottom right: Soweto, South Africa, June 1976. Police fire on student demonstration of 10,000, sparking mass upsurge that accelerated struggle leading to overthrow of apartheid regime in early 1990s.

Top: Tehran, March 8, 1979. Thousands of women, who were part of insurrection that toppled shah a month before, call for equal rights and protest new regime's efforts to force women in Iran to wear veil.

Middle: Managua, Nicaragua, July 1979. US-backed Somoza dictatorship was overturned by popular revolutionary movement.

Bottom: Grenada, 1980. Working people rally to protest Washington's threats to revolutionary government that came to power in March 1979.

"As the bosses and their government increasingly target industrial workers and their unions, the rulers are pushing this decisive sector of our class toward the center stage of US politics."

Top: Washington, DC, April 1975. Supporters of Steelworkers Fight Back—organized by ranks fighting for union democracy—join AFL-CIO rally for jobs.

Bottom: Wellington, New Zealand, June 1976. Rally of 10,000 protests wage freeze. Opponents of apartheid regime in South Africa joined action, as did students protesting cuts in education and a contingent calling for legalization of abortion.

CHRIS HORNER/MILITANT

AUGUST 3, 1979   50 CENTS   VOLUME 43/NUMBER 30

THE MILITANT

A SOCIALIST NEWSWEEKLY PUBLISHED IN THE INTERESTS OF THE WORKING PEOPLE

New advances for Cuban revolution

Oklahoma auto workers score victory for all labor

Organizing drive defeats GM conspiracy

OKLAHOMA CITY—Union members cheer election triumph. See page 3.

AUGUST 3, 1979

ANDY ROSE/MILITANT

Top: Oklahoma City, July 1979. Auto workers celebrate 2-to-1 win against General Motors in union organizing drive. Along with the successful drive by Steelworkers in Newport News—the biggest in the South in a quarter century—victory gave boost to working-class struggles everywhere.

Bottom: Virginia, Minnesota, August 1977. Some 18,000 striking Steelworkers shut down iron ore mines and production plants in Minnesota's Iron Range and in Michigan.

"We use the *Militant*, books, and SWP election campaigns to explain the truth about capitalist exploitation, oppression, and wars—and how working people are resisting assaults on our rights and conditions of life and work."

MILITANT

Left: Dan Fein, steelworker and SWP candidate for mayor of Phoenix, Arizona, in 1979.

WEST VIRGINIA AND REGIONAL HISTORY CENTER

MILITANT

Middle: Tom Moriarty, coal miner and candidate for governor of West Virginia in 1980. "Miners have proven we can fight and win," said Moriarty. "So let's do it in politics as well as on the picket line."

Bottom: Eli Green and Cappy Kidd, both shipyard workers, ran for city council in Newport News, Virginia, in 1982.

Left: Kiruna, Sweden, February 1999. Introducing the *Militant* to a miner at LKAB iron ore complex, 90 miles above Arctic Circle.

"The *Militant* has great leverage," says Barnes. "Each issue reports—in workers' own voices, and in our own names—about resistance to the capitalists in factories, mines, and working-class communities."

The SWP organized a leadership school "to help elected party leaders reeducate themselves in our Marxist program through concentrated study." Ten six-month sessions were organized from 1980 to 1986. **Above,** participants in spring 1981 class.

"In the 1974–75 Boston desegregation struggle, the Black community and its supporters fought the racists to a standoff."

Above: Boston, December 1974. "Keep the buses rolling," thousands chanted in demonstration supporting desegregation of Boston's public schools. When Democratic Party leaders organized thugs to assault school buses, the attacks were beaten back by mass meetings, demonstrations, and organization of bus marshals.

That battle, Barnes says, "was the single most decisive political combat experience for an entire layer of the party leadership, including a big component of our leadership who are Black."

"It's through the *Militant* and books we publish that co-workers learn who we are. We're supporters of Black rights and women's equality. We defend the Cuban Revolution. We think workers should control safety and production."

Rail workers under attack

By Dick Roberts

Railroad workers set protest

Milwaukee Rd. bankruptcy: owners plan ripoff

By Dick Roberts

SEPTEMBER 29, 1978

AUGUST 3, 1979

STOP MILWAUKEE SHUTDOWN

INVESTIGATE MILWAUKEEGATE

In 1977 Milwaukee Road rail bosses were among first freight carriers to use bankruptcy courts to cut crew sizes, lay off workers, and boost profits. Rail workers put out buttons and T-shirts demanding "Investigate Milwaukeegate."

Top: Minneapolis, June 1979. Meeting of 250 demands bosses "Open the books!" Six rail union locals endorsed action, attended by workers from as far away as Oregon and Idaho.

Right: *Militant* campaigned weekly in defense of rail jobs and safety.

"We stand with the coal miners who have pushed back black lung since the 1960s and won community health clinics. Who formed Miners for Democracy so they could wield union power to defend the ranks."

The UMWA, then the most powerful union in US, was a special target of rulers' drive to bust labor movement. **Above:** Washington, DC, March 1981. Miners hold national protest a few weeks before 160,000 began 10-week strike, turning back concession contract demanded by coal bosses—as they had done during 110-day strike in 1977–78.

workers. That is how trade union work has to be understood.

We don't need a day-to-day balance sheet of the individual ups and downs of this work. We don't judge by the dry periods, when less can be done. We go by the long-run effort of the party and the fractions, on a nationwide scale. That is the only possible way to measure the accomplishments of trade union work. What individual comrades can do will vary greatly—from one time to another in the same job, and from one job to another in the same industry.

Trade union work must not be seen as separate from party campaigns. It's not "another campaign" somewhere in the list of priorities. It's our axis, our milieu, and our basic arena of work. It strengthens all our campaigns, as it strengthens the work of the Young Socialist Alliance.

We've already learned some lessons from our work in steel and other industries. One is that we don't have to sit around waiting for big struggles to occur before we can do something. Struggles are coming. But they're not happening in every single place, at all times, for all comrades.

While we don't have to wait, we also can't begin with the idea we're going to stir up big struggles if they are not occurring. Our size precludes that. As long as we avoid these two errors, we can do an immense amount of work.

We have to ask ourselves another question about trade union work. What would the party be missing if we were not to get into industry in our big majority, *today*? Not after our next national gathering, not after the next meeting of the National Committee, but *today*.

One of the main things we'd miss would be learning the life of the working class in a rich way. We'd miss having our fingers on the pulse of the changes beginning to take place in politics in the United States. We'd miss learning the life of the factories, the mills, and the mines. We'd miss learning the life of the unions, and life in bureaucratically degenerated, declining unions. We'd miss being part of the life of workers, the rhythms, the problems, the experiences, the difficulties.

All this can really be known only one way—by being there. Once we're there, we don't need fake Gallup polls to try to figure out what workers are thinking.

Farrell [Dobbs] reminded me of a story about Lenin during the July Days in Russia in 1917, when Lenin had been forced by government threats of arrest to go underground. A worker says, "They're afraid of us, Comrade Lenin."

Lenin asks, "What have you heard, comrade?"

The worker replies, "The bread is better."

Lenin didn't need a poll. He didn't have to wait for the Petrograd Gallup to come out, which could be fake and wrong. A party of worker-bolsheviks is the best poll.

The key thing for us is the fruitful party-building work to be done right now in the center of political life in the United States—the industrial working class. By center, of course, we're not saying this is the only place. There are not big political street actions taking place. But more and more, what happens in the unions and to the unions deeply affects the entire relationship of class forces. It's here that the leadership, the future class-struggle leadership of all the movements of the oppressed and exploited is being forged and has to be forged if they are to be led to victory.

Thus, changing the composition of the party becomes the source of a great strengthening of the party. We'll not only have our fingers directly on the pulse of the key sections of the American working class, but we'll get to know workers, including ourselves, who are being tested and trained to become leaders in coming battles. This is the single most important arena of training for the proletarian leaders of the struggles ahead.

A party of worker-bolsheviks

What is a worker-bolshevik?—a term we proudly take from Lenin. What is a party whose big majority are worker-bolsheviks?

As an individual, a worker-bolshevik is somebody who is a member of a revolutionary party of workers, a party known by workers, a party that knows workers. A party trusted by other workers—and trusting *in* other workers. A party made up, in its ranks and leadership, of workers. Very simple. But there is more.

A worker-bolshevik is a worker for whom the party comes first. A worker for whom the party is everything. We're in industry, in the unions, for one ultimate reason: to build the party. This will be the arena of battle where the party will either win the leadership among the oppressed and exploited in the battle for power, or lose leadership to one of the petty-bourgeois currents and see the counterrevolution triumph. That is why we're in the unions and why we are going to be in them deeper and deeper.

Worker-bolsheviks are professional revolutionists in the best sense of the term. As we know, professional revolutionists are not the same thing as full-timers, although they are ready at any moment to shoulder a full-time assignment at the request of the party. Regardless of how he or she makes enough money to live on, a worker-bolshevik is someone who at all times takes on major responsibility as a member of the party, in whatever way is necessary. A comrade who sustains financially and supports politically the full-time apparatus of the party, the press, the political infrastructure the party needs to function.

A worker-bolshevik is ready to move—into a new industry or a new city—when the need arises. Ready to aid the expansion of the party, making it possible to become stronger nationwide, making it possible to respond to a political opening such as in Morgantown, West Virginia, or on the Iron Range in Minnesota. Ready to pitch in and build the branches we've started in important political centers—centers that affect whole regions and states—such as Albany, Raleigh, Salt Lake City, Miami, San Antonio, and Toledo, branches that need reinforcements if they are going to be able to take advantage of the openings.

To underline this point, the leadership is obligated to praise pyromania.

One of my favorite quotes from Jim Cannon is from his summary speech to the party plenum-conference in 1941. He was talking about colonizing industry, as we are doing today, and said there was nothing "more disgraceful for a young revolutionist than to get settled down and get so encumbered" that the comrade no longer wanted to move. "It would be a damn good thing for him if he had a fire" to blow away some property encumbrance and become "footloose and revolutionary again."[15]

That should be put up on the wall in the home of every worker-bolshevik. It's the truth.

When workers join the party, they see their co-workers serving on branch and local executive committees, on forum committees, as financial and education directors, as SWP campaign organizers and candidates for public office, and so on. If this were not normal in a party of worker-bolsheviks, then the whole concept would be a utopia.

A worker-bolshevik is a comrade who doesn't believe that you do political activity only after you get off work. They don't wait to get away from their job, or find a job that

---

15. Cannon, *The Socialist Workers Party in World War II*, p. 237.

makes them "available" for other things but minimizes the opportunities for political work on the job.

Worker-bolsheviks see themselves as socialist propagandists on the job and off. They sell the *Militant*. They sell books and pamphlets. They raise ideas about leading the class struggle, opposed to the class-collaborationist policies of the current leadership. They are talking continually to workers about politics, about our campaigns, about our paper, about getting to know other revolutionists, about supporting social struggles of mass protest that need the support of labor.

Last, *but most important*, they talk with fellow workers about joining the party.

A party structure

What about a party of worker-bolsheviks from the point of view of party norms and structure?

The key thing, once again, is that the party must lead. The party can never leave a fraction on its own. An industrial union fraction is not a fraction of Steelworkers Fight Back, or some caucus of the UMWA, or of the Oil, Chemical and Atomic Workers. It is a fraction of Socialist Workers Party members. And above all else, this fraction of the Socialist Workers Party must be led in harmony with the rhythm of the class struggle and the character and pace of the party campaigns we take into the unions. This points to a series of adjustments that will become norms in the party.

The relationship of the industrial fractions to the branches and the locals must be developed through our experience. The specific forms will vary. In some places, for example in Houston, we have trade union directors working in collaboration with all the fractions as part of the city leadership. In other places, such as the Bay Area, we use ad hoc forms. We have a Bay Area–wide steel fraction, which a National Committee member helps lead. We will find the best forms and use them.

This turn to the industrial working class and unions affects everything we do, every aspect of our structure and functioning. Branch meeting times have to change so comrades working in industry can attend. Branch sizes have to be reevaluated. We have to look at sales of the *Militant* and *Perspectiva Mundial* in this framework. Sales at plant gates on a regular, consistent basis are going to be essential as part of providing outside help for the fractions inside the plants.

The party has to lead by putting comrades in industry. This must be a conscious, organized campaign. And the leadership leads by setting the example. It has to become the norm that the majority of executive committees members are in industry. We have to enable comrades who are branch and city organizers to do this—and, at the same time, bring forward a new layer of comrades to get the experience of being organizers. We are releasing members of the National Committee from other assignments to go into industry now. Members of the trade union steering committee and some members of the Political Committee will do so as well.

We must also put greater stress now on education. Like the working class itself, worker-bolsheviks have a great need and a great thirst for education. We have to read, think, listen, discuss. We have to learn how to explain things, and read to keep up with our co-workers.

We have to pay attention to local and branch educational programs. We have to think through how best to use our national educational conferences each year. We have to seriously consider restarting something like the Trotsky School,[16] to provide a systematic way to take elected party

---

16. See glossary: Trotsky School; SWP leadership school.

leaders out of their day-to-day responsibilities—members of the National Committee and the Political Committee to start with—and help them to educate and reeducate themselves in our Marxist program through concentrated study for four or five months.

But the key thing is to act *now* to get the majority of the party and the majority of the leadership into industry. That's the great opportunity, the responsibility of leadership.

Once industrial workers are a big majority of a branch, the rhythms and the needs of the majority of comrades become the norm. Only when this is not the case do organizational questions about the relations between branches and union fractions become problems. Life teaches that the average comrade doesn't become a less active trade unionist but a more active bolshevik.

The changes we must make in our structure will come naturally and be seen not as problems but as a normal part of party life, of taking advantage of opportunities as we succeed in transforming the party. As this happens, a new norm is established. You forget what was normal yesterday. What becomes normal is what is normal today.

Leadership lessons

Our sixth and final question: What is the leadership of this kind of party like?

We have a new, relatively young National Committee. But it has one of the biggest responsibilities, maybe the biggest opportunity, of any national leadership in the history of the party. So we wanted to take a little time in this part of the report to discuss this question of questions—*leadership*.

If the party is going to lead a proletarian revolution, it has to be a proletarian party. It has to be a proletarian party in program, in composition, in experience, and in its leadership. It must understand the epoch it is in. Its task is not one of reforming capitalism. Our perspective is the elimination of capitalist rule. Our program is socialist revolution.

We don't have a bunch of programs for different sections or layers of the working class. We reject any concept of sectoralism or polyvanguardism. The way forward is that of a proletarian revolution, and the vanguard has to be the organized, conscious vanguard of the proletariat. The most powerful, centralized ruling class in history has to be displaced.

That doesn't end the matter, however, because the proletariat is not homogeneous. If the proletariat—which is the big majority—were totally homogeneous, if every worker went through the same experiences and came to the same conclusions at the same time, a conscious, politically homogeneous combat party wouldn't be so necessary. We might slip by with the broadest class institutions—factory committees, soviets, whatever—which by definition encompass the great active majority of the whole class.

But in reality, just when that stage is reached—the stage of the transformation of the gigantic industrial unions into revolutionary instruments of struggle, the establishment of workers councils, the establishment of soviets—it's just at that point that the heterogeneous character of the class (based on historic differences along lines of craft, race, sex, age, and political experience) makes the need for the party so acute.

A party is needed that will speak for the most conscious sections of the proletariat, and lead the fight to oppose and win the least conscious and the most backward toilers, those most affected by bourgeois and petty-bourgeois ideology. Thus, it is not a matter of indifference whether the party is rooted in, and a significant part of its leadership and membership is composed of, sections of the working class that are doubly oppressed in capitalist society. These workers will be among the best fighters and the most courageous, resolute, and conscious leaders of the party and of the class.

The rise of the Black rights movement and of the women's struggle have had a great impact, a historical impact we've often discussed. But they have one meaning above all others for the revolutionary party: the human material, the potential leaders of the proletarian party, have been expanded.

If this is true, it says something else. All leaders *lead the party*, not a sector of the party or a grouping in the party. Naturally, leaders who are women are looked to by younger women in the party as examples, as people to learn from. The same with comrades who are Black. We all go through this experience. When you find someone like yourself, with whom you can identify, it helps you develop the confidence to take strides forward.

But what we are after is not Black leaders of the party. We need party leaders who are Black. Not Chicano leaders of the party, or women leaders of the party, or worker leaders of the party, but rounded leaders—looked to by the entire party—who are Black, Chicano, Puerto Rican, female, and industrial workers.

Not leaders who take responsibility for only one section of the party, or one area of work, but leaders who take overall responsibility, who lead the work of the entire party.

The decision we're making at this meeting of the National Committee has an important bearing on the development of such leadership, because the industrial working class is where proletarian leadership will be fostered. Industry will not be the only place, since struggles by working people and the oppressed occur among other exploited layers in cities, small towns, rural areas, and other work-places. But it is primarily in industry that our leaders will gain experience and confidence and come forward. This is universal, for the party as a whole.

No different roads

We do not have different roads to leadership. We cannot have different roads for Caucasian and Black, male and fe-male, more and less experienced cadres. If we had different criteria, then leadership elections would become a fraud.

Our work in industry, and getting into industry, is the central leadership responsibility of all cadres. This is where the next leadership of the proletarian party historically, and the leaders of the next stage of the mass movement, will come from.

It is true not only for the future class-struggle left wing in the unions, but for the Black movement, the Chicano movement, the Puerto Rican movement, the women's movement. If those struggles are to advance, it's from here and not from the ranks of lawyers, preachers, professors, labor fakers, petty-bourgeois politicians, and ex–govern-ment officials that leaders will come. They are going to be found among the American working class, and that is where we have to be to win them.

There is another side to this, too. In thinking about this report I went back and read *The Struggle for a Proletarian Party*. I was struck by something I hadn't remembered so much from earlier readings: the stress that Jim Cannon put on *attitudes* toward leadership and organization.

He listed a lot of the characteristics of proletarian lead-ers. *Seriousness* toward the organization of the leadership. *Objectivity*. Subordinating personal considerations and *putting the party first*. Having a *professional attitude* toward it. Being deadly opposed to gossip, cynicism, bureaucratism, hypersensitivity to criticism. All these traits, Jim stressed, are proletarian attitudes toward the party.

That wasn't only Cannon's view. It was Trotsky's, as well, based on the experience of Lenin and the Bolsheviks. Trotsky's praise of *The Struggle for a Proletarian Party* as "the writing of a genuine workers leader"—and his polemical articles and letters on leadership and organization in *In Defense of Marxism*—made the same point. We incorporated this view as part of the fundamental program of the SWP, including our 1965 resolution on party norms and principles, *The Organizational Character of the Socialist Workers Party*.

Above all, *objectivity is the key to this.* To lead and set an example on the organization question, on the leadership question, above all we have to be objective, not subjective. The starting point is never "me and mine" but "us and ours"—the needs of the party, the needs of the working class.

Steelworkers fight
to take back their union

In early 1977 Jack Barnes toured nine cities—from Pittsburgh and Cleveland to Houston, Chicago, Detroit, and the San Francisco Bay Area—speaking with workers about the Steelworkers Fight Back movement.[1]

Fight Back leader Ed Sadlowski, president of USWA District 31 in Chicago and northwest Indiana, was running for USWA president that year to oust the officialdom of I.W. Abel, which was working hand in glove with the steel bosses. Abel resigned rather than face the challenge, handpicking his lieutenant Lloyd McBride to replace him.

The other candidates on the Fight Back ticket were Oliver Montgomery, vice-president (human affairs); Marvin Weinstock, vice-president (administration); Nash Rodriguez, secretary; Andrew Kmec, treasurer; and Jim Balanoff, who was elected District 31 president. In the vote, held February

---

1. See glossary: Steelworkers Fight Back; Experimental Negotiating Agreement; USWA.

7, 1977, Sadlowski was credited with 238,150 votes, McBride with 324,500.

An interview with Barnes on the significance of Steelworkers Fight Back appeared in the April 8 and April 15, 1977, issues of the *Militant*. Excerpts from Barnes's answers to the reporter's questions are reprinted below.

Union democracy, the right to strike, the need for a union that stands up against the boss—those were the decisive issues for the Steelworkers Fight Back movement.

The fact that there were nearly a quarter of a million votes for the Sadlowski team *that were counted* points to the real victory—the beginning mobilization of thousands of steelworkers in a fight to take back their union. That was Fight Back's victory.

The way steelworkers divided in the vote was not, as often reported, small shops versus basic steel, but according to their relative privileges, their age, and their political attitudes.

Sadlowski carried the vote in many smaller shops—which have lower wage scales, worse conditions, and worse union representation than basic steel—where the ideas of Fight Back had been gotten out.

Sadlowski apparently did win a majority in basic steel—which is extremely significant as a vote of no-confidence in the Abel leadership. It's a vote to repudiate the no-strike Experimental Negotiating Agreement in basic steel.

But McBride often carried the most skilled, high-seniority, relatively privileged workers. That's what one would expect when such basic class questions were being posed.

The second factor was the lack of literature dealing directly with the problems of Black, Chicano, and women workers. I'm convinced this hurt Fight Back.

Where the Sadlowski slate spoke—and where Black,

"Union democracy, the right to strike, a union that stands up against the boss—those were the decisive issues for the Steelworkers Fight Back movement."

Top: Ed Sadlowski, Steelworkers Fight Back candidate for union president, speaks at Detroit rally, February 5, 1977. "Fight Back supported steps to combat discrimination against Blacks, Chicanos, and women on the job, in the union, and in society," Barnes says.

Inset: Leaflet for Fight Back slate.

Bottom: Sadlowski campaigns at US Steel's South Works, Chicago, August 1976. Campaign was used by ranks to challenge entrenched USWA bureaucracy and seek democratic control of their union.

"Fighting miners won union safety committees able to shut down production over unsafe conditions and, through Miners for Democracy, won right to vote on contracts."

ROBERT GUMPERT/APPALSHOP ARCHIVE

Top: Charleston, West Virginia, February 26, 1969. Coal miners demand action against black lung. After strike by 40,000 miners, governor signed law requiring companies to pay compensation for crippling disease. Black lung mobilizations gave rise to Miners for Democracy movement, which won greater control of union by the ranks.

Bottom: Harlan County, Kentucky, 1974. Miners rally during hard-fought strike to win UMWA representation at a Duke Power mine. Successful fight won nationwide attention, galvanizing support after company foreman killed a young striker.

NANCY COLE/MILITANT

MILITANT

JACOB PERASSO/MILITANT

Top: Striking coal miners march in Washington, DC, March 1978. Some 160,000 coal miners waged 110-day strike, beating back coal bosses' concession demands. They defied Carter administration's back-to-work order invoked under Taft-Hartley Act.

Center: April 1977. At steel plants across US, socialist workers sold 4,000 copies of *Militant* issue with full official summary of new USWA contract.

Bottom right: Galatia, Illinois, November 2011. Selling socialist press outside mine portal. Regular *Militant* sales at plant gates are "essential as part of providing outside help for party fractions inside the plants," Barnes explains.

> "Trade union work, properly understood, means finding ways to advance the development of a mass working-class vanguard that thinks socially and acts politically."

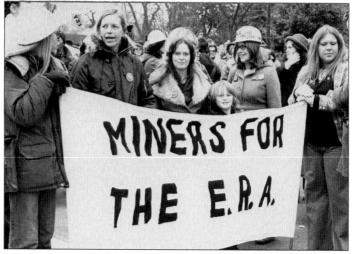

NANCY COLE/MILITANT

'End U.S. aid to So. Africa'
Black trade unionist begins United States tour

Drake Koka, general secretary of the Black Allied Workers Union (BAWU) of South Africa, began a seven-week tour of the United States on October 2. He is speaking about political prisoners in South Africa and the fight for Black majority rule.

Koka has been indicted by the South African government as a "co-conspirator" in the frame-up trial of eleven Soweto student leaders charged with "sedition" and "terrorism." That trial is now under way in the town of Kempton Park, near Johannesburg.

BAWU was founded in August 1972. Its purpose, according to Koka, is "to organize a united, powerful African workers union."

Koka was also a cofounder and first general secretary of the Black People's Convention, an umbrella organization that developed out of the Black Consciousness Movement. In October 1977 it was outlawed along with other major Black groups by the South African government.

In February 1973 the apartheid regime placed Koka under a five-year ban that kept him under house arrest. He was arrested and jailed for eight months during 1974-75.

After participating in the June 1976 Soweto rebellion, Koka was again banned. He escaped to Botswana to avoid arrest.

Below is the text of a press release issued by the Drake Koka Tour Committee upon his arrival in the United States.

I am glad that I am here again in the United States. My last visit was in October 1977.

whose trend of thought is "shoot first and then ask questions"—shows the arrogant determination of the Afrikaners never to give up their oppressive, exploitative apartheid policy. Their determination never to hand over power to the Black majority.

DRAKE KOKA: 'Our demand is Black majority rule'

Hear Drake Koka
Drake Koka will be speaking in the following cities during October.

Oct. 6-9 Cleveland
10-11 Newark
12-14 New York
16-19 Boston/Western Massachusetts
20 Midwest Conference on South Africa, Evanston, Ill.
21 New York State NAACP conference, Newburgh
22-24 Detroit
26-27 Baltimore/Washington, D.C.

The tour committee has also received many new endorsers.

These include: Patrick Gorman, chairman of the board of the Amalgamated Meat Cutters and Butcher Workmen of North America; Tom Turner, president, Metro Detroit Central Labor Council; Ralph David Abernathy, president emeritus, Southern Christian Leadership Conference; Michael Harrington, national chairperson, Democratic Socialist Organizing Committee; David McReynolds, War Resisters League.

Also Osleyo Ayago, chairperson, Pan African Studies Department, Temple University; Black Leadership Caucus, Cleveland Federation of Labor; Sonia Sanchez, poet and novelist; Pete Camarata, Teamsters for a Democratic Union; Black American Law Student Association chapters at the University of Louisville, and Rutgers

MILITANT, OCTOBER 13, 1978

Top: Richmond, Virginia, January 1980. UMWA contingent in union-sponsored march of 5,000 for ratification of Equal Rights Amendment. Holding banner are leaders of the Coal Employment Project, which helped women get mining jobs.

Bottom: Launching of US speaking tour by South African unionist Drake Koka, who explained place of trade unions in fight against apartheid regime. Miners in West Virginia, including socialist workers, helped build a meeting for Koka.

Chicano, and women workers went and posed the tough questions—Fight Back leaders laid out pretty good answers. They stood for equal representation of minorities and women in the union leadership and staff. They supported a series of specific steps against discrimination on the job and in the union. They said the union power should be used to fight discrimination and segregation throughout society.

But the lack of literature directly addressing these needs, the failure to put this appeal to the most oppressed workers in the forefront of the Fight Back campaign—this hurt.

If the Sadlowski slate had won, they were convinced—not only by the speeches of the Sadlowski team but by their own experiences—that new people in office alone wouldn't solve a thing in the Steelworkers union. Only the mobilization and organization of the ranks would do this.

In some ways the most important challenge before the Steelworkers Fight Back leadership is their willingness now to continue and organize in the confidence that they can attract not only the hundreds of thousands who voted for them but the millions more who they will reach.

What is important is to find a way to continue a national focus. Up to February 8 the national focus was the election. Now the Fight Back leaders have to find a new focus—a publication, a response to conditions in the mills, a response to the bosses' offensive that is going to keep coming down around jobs, wages, conditions, and victimization of militant steelworkers.

The direction of the movement is to reach out to workers in other industries. A Fight Back movement is needed in every union in this country.

This fight for union democracy, and the fight for workers' interests against the employers, will get a hearing as more and more conflicts arise. The conditions in this country, and the incapacity of the employers to give the kind of concessions that they gave in the past, are going to make millions and millions of American workers ready to fight back.

〜

In Pittsburgh, I went to hear Abel's final campaign speech. He truly believes that the only salvation for the union— which he identifies with himself and his kind—is to make common cause with the bosses and rely on their goodwill.

Here is his view of unionism: "We contribute as well as receive. We are not a 'give me' organization. We had the well-earned reputation of being strike-happy.[2] The ENA settled that."

Apparently Abel thinks strikes took place because the union demanded too much, a view he undoubtedly picked up from the steel executives he hangs around with.

It was also clear from his speech how deeply the question of foreign imports is tied up with the no-strike deal. Here's how he put it: "Foreign imports are the greatest danger to our well-being and national security. The ENA was the answer to this threat. The purpose of the ENA is to stabilize our industry and to safeguard our markets."

You can see how Abel identifies completely with the interests of the capitalists. *Our* industry . . . *our* markets . . . *our* national security. That's the voice of steel *bosses*, not steel *workers*. . . .

Abel shares the capitalist disdain for workers. He used his speech to ridicule Sadlowski's statements on their intellectual capacities.

---

2. Abel is referring to the 116-day strike by 450,000 steelworkers in 1959, the biggest action in the US between the post–World War II labor upsurge and the renewed fight in the coalfields in the 1970s.

"These people say steelworkers are capable of becoming doctors, songwriters, and poets." Abel said this with a tone of heavy sarcasm, as if only a total fool could think such a thing.

This is "irresponsible."

That's the mentality and the program of the bureaucracy: Total collaboration with the employers, "our" industry against foreigners, defense of the capitalist system.

The bureaucracy has done its best to wipe out the idea that you can fight the employers and use union power to defeat them.

Fight Back has begun turning this around. But many workers still have to learn in struggle that you can make gains by fighting back.

When American workers do take over their unions and use them as instruments of struggle for *their* class interests, they will be the greatest power on earth.

Twenty-five lessons:
The first year of the turn

The following are major excerpts from a report adopted by delegates to the August 5–11, 1979, Socialist Workers Party convention. The vote was 121 to 1. The report by Jack Barnes drew on the first year and half of practical political experience by a new generation of party members in the industrial working class and unions engaging in labor and social struggles of all kinds.

I.

At our February 1978 National Committee meeting, we voted to lead the party into industry. We decided to immediately organize the great majority of members and leaders of the Socialist Workers Party into industrial jobs and industrial unions in order to do political work as part of the decisive sectors of our class.

Underlying this decision was our estimate of the state of the world economy and changes in world politics following the defeat for US imperialism in Vietnam and the 1974–75 worldwide recession. For the first time since the late 1940s, the economic and political changes in this country—including the new shoots of combativity and class consciousness among American workers, and the consequent increase in class polarization—produced an opportunity for the SWP to do political work in the weightiest sectors of our class. We decided to subordinate everything to getting ourselves into position to make the most of that opening.

Reviewing the progress of our turn to industry over the past year and a half, as well as national and world events, the Political Committee drafted the political resolution before the delegates to this convention. In May 1979 the National Committee unanimously adopted the resolution and submitted it to branches for discussion and vote as the basis for the election of convention delegates.[1] That resolution reviews the world political situation as it affects US politics and vice versa. It reviews the continuity of our political program and course throughout the radicalization of the past two decades, and the lessons we've learned from the initial experiences of our growing trade union fractions.

The party has now had several months of discussion and debate, both in written form in the internal bulletin and in weekly branch meetings. A counterresolution submitted by several comrades, entitled "Against the Workerist Turn: A Critique and Some Proposals," has also been before our members. We've had one of the richest preconvention discussions in years, drawing on the party's concrete, practical experience in the industrial working class and unions. At this convention, comrades will have further discussion,

---

1. An excerpt from that 1979 resolution, "Building a Revolutionary Party of Socialist Workers," can be found in *The Changing Face of US Politics* by Jack Barnes.

vote on the party's course, and elect a National Committee to lead its implementation.

To obtain maximum clarity on the central disputed political questions before the delegates, we will boil them down to twenty-five points that capture the heart of the party's political course.

Vietnam and US imperialism's decline

One. The Vietnam War changed American politics from top to bottom. What was previously considered impossible—even unthinkable—*happened.*

It happened in a prolonged and painful way. Painful for the ruling class, who could not believe it. And painful for the working class, who paid the price in blood for the class arrogance of the employers. It more and more happened before the eyes of the entire American population via television. It happened to the sons, fathers, nephews, husbands, and neighbors of millions and millions of Americans.

And slowly but surely, the American working class consciously reached some conclusions. Since US combat troops were pulled out of Southeast Asia in 1973, "No more Vietnams!" has become perhaps the most popular single slogan in this country.

This suspicion of US foreign policy and unwillingness to fight Washington's wars has been reinforced by the so-called Watergate revelations in the early 1970s of wiretapping and burglary by the Richard Nixon White House against its capitalist political opponents. Those exposures put a spotlight on secret FBI and other government spying and disruption operations under both Democratic and Republican administrations against the labor movement, opponents of imperialist wars, fighters for Black freedom and women's emancipation, and the Communist Party, Socialist Workers Party, and other organizations identified as communist.

These political police operations got their biggest initial thrust during the Franklin Roosevelt New Deal and War Deal years.[2] The assaults culminated in the indictment and imprisonment of leaders of the Socialist Workers Party and Midwest Teamster leaders for their campaign in the labor movement to oppose US imperialist war aims and wage freezes, no-strike pledges, and other antilabor measures by the capitalist rulers and their allies to hogtie the unions in the name of national unity.[3]

∾

Two. The continuing impact of Washington's defeat in Vietnam has a direct bearing on one of the biggest factors in world politics: the mounting obstacles the US rulers face in wielding their military power against the workers and toiling masses around the world in the way they've been accustomed to doing.

Over the past half decade, there have been victories and advances for our class in Grenada; in Nicaragua; in Iran; in Vietnam, Kampuchea, and Laos; in Angola and the other

---

2. Elected at the rock bottom of the Great Depression, Roosevelt in 1933–34 initiated what he called the New Deal, a package of reforms aimed at corralling and defusing the mighty rise of working-class resistance, which posed a threat to capitalist rule. The New Deal's promise of ending the capitalist crisis and reversing widespread joblessness, however, only began to take hold as it grew into the War Deal at the end of the 1930s and then US entry into the imperialist Second World War itself in December 1941.

3. On December 8, 1941, eighteen leaders of Local 544-CIO and of the Socialist Workers Party, convicted in federal court of "conspiracy to advocate the overthrow of the US government," were given sentences ranging from twelve to sixteen months in prison. These were the first convictions under the Smith "Gag" Act, signed into law by Roosevelt in June 1940.

former Portuguese colonies; in Ethiopia.[4] The capacity of the toiling masses in the colonial world to snap back from defeats and the brutal repression of vicious regimes, and to battle and overthrow their oppressors, has been demonstrated time and again.

We could not have asked for a more inspiring or convincing example than the Nicaraguan people, who—a little more than two weeks ago, on July 19, in the face of ruthless violence by the regime's National Guard—drove the tyrant Anastasio Somoza and Somozaism out of their land.

American imperialism has discovered that the junior partners it counts on—the so-called surrogates, the reactionary figures such as Somoza and the shah of Iran—are less and less able to hold back the class struggle for their imperial masters, and for themselves.

We've witnessed the growing preponderance of the proletariat and semiproletarian urban masses in the revolutionary upheavals in these countries. Nearly 39 percent of the world's population lives in urban areas in 1978, up from 31 percent only a quarter century ago.[5]

It is the very advances of the neocolonial bourgeoisies under the tutelage of imperialism, their need to extract surplus value, that accelerate the ruination of toilers on the land and foster the growth of a proletariat that then turns around and bites its creators. That's what the bourgeoisie calls ingratitude!

Despite these political limitations, US imperialism remains world capitalism's only strategic military power. Washington's military budget and the size and diversity

---

4. See glossary: Grenada Revolution (1978–83); Nicaraguan Revolution; Iranian Revolution; Vietnam; Cambodia; Angola; Ethiopian Revolution (1974).

5. In 2018, some 55 percent of the world's population lived in cities and large towns.

of its conventional weaponry and nuclear arsenal continue to grow. Withdrawal of American combat units from South Korea is postponed.[6] New nuclear-armed strike forces are announced. Proposals to reestablish selective service registration and the draft proliferate in Washington.[7] Trial balloons are sent up to see how far aggression can be pushed—an aircraft carrier off Indochina; "advisers" and warships to Yemen and the Arab Gulf; talk of protecting "our" oil reserves in Saudi Arabia.

Underneath all this, the ultimate contradiction facing American imperialism remains. It must be able to intervene militarily around the world in order to respond to revolutionary challenges to capitalist rule. But to do so, the rulers have to take on the American working class, which less and less sees a clear stake in Washington's military adventures abroad. This contradiction is a weighty one in world politics.[8]

~

Three. The political crisis for the bourgeoisie limiting its use of American military power occurs within the frame-

---

6. In 1979, when this report was adopted, 39,000 US troops were deployed in South Korea. Forty years later there are still 28,500 troops there—the third-largest US deployment abroad, following Japan and Germany.

7. Military conscription itself, which became a target of mass opposition among workers and youth during the Vietnam War, was ended in 1973 under the Republican administration of Richard Nixon. Draft registration for all eligible men ages 19 and 20, however, was reestablished in July 1980 by the Democratic administration of James Carter and Congress.

8. The evolution of US imperialist military policy over the quarter century after this report was adopted is detailed in the 2005 SWP resolution, "Their Transformation and Ours" (issue no. 12 of *New International* magazine).

work of the developing crisis of US and world capitalism that came to the surface in the early 1970s.

Economic crisis of capitalism

The international capitalist system has entered a long period tending toward economic stagnation, with occasional bursts of explosive inflation. The broad capitalist expansion that marked most of the quarter century following World War II is behind us. Superimposed on this economic stagnation is a growing tendency for social and political crises to break out even in the most stable capitalist countries, unsettling the social relations of capitalism.

Of course, American capitalism can and does still make concessions to working people. It can, it has, and it will make more as the class struggle advances. But there is no possibility of major, stable economic concessions such as a gigantic new extension of social security.

Over the past decade we've gone from steady inflation that picked up speed as the Vietnam War escalated, to the antilabor offensive launched by US imperialism in 1971—Nixon's wage freeze and other measures to "zap labor."

That was followed in 1973 by the rigged meat and oil shortages across the United States. Prices soared at meat counters. Drivers suffered blocks-long lines at gas stations, and then, when they filled up their tanks, it was at higher and higher prices. And workers had to put up with cold or completely unheated apartments and houses for much of the winter. Inflation reached into the double digits, followed by the 1974–75 worldwide downturn, setting off the biggest round of layoffs and attacks on workers' living standards since Washington's entry into World War II.[9]

---

9. See glossary: Wage-price freeze (1971); Recession (1974–75).

The ruling-class offensive is aimed at weakening the main class organizations of American workers—our unions. The employers aim to increase their rate of profit by intensifying the exploitation of workers, so they must go after the industrial unions. They have no other choice.

This does not mean that the immediate goal of the capitalists is to destroy the industrial unions. When the bosses and their government feel tactically ready to do that, you won't have to be told about it at an SWP convention or read about it in a resolution. But *right now* the employers are aiming to systematically weaken, undercut, and drive back the industrial unions in any way they can. They are probing to see how much they can take back, how far they can go in attacking the most powerful organized sections of the American working class.

That has been the policy of the American ruling class for nearly a decade, and they've been accelerating its implementation since 1975.

Without a fight to transform the industrial unions into revolutionary instruments of class struggle, there is no way for our class to prevent the social breakdowns, catastrophes, the gnawing uncertainties and insecurity, the threat of imperialist wars, that come down more and more heavily on working people.

The ruling class can't simply plan in advance what to do—when to push harder, when to pull back. They don't exercise control of the economy; capitalism is an anarchic system. The bosses face mounting competition at home and abroad, as well as growing uncertainties and often spiraling problems of their own. They are by necessity pragmatic, driven to weigh the short run over the long run. Economic and social forces are not only out of *our* control, but often beyond the control of the very capitalists whose necessary actions set those forces in motion.

~

Four. There is a growing realization among American workers that good times don't lie ahead. This changing consciousness didn't develop overnight.

The capitalist takeback offensive at first struck particularly hard at social services and at teachers and other public employees, most notoriously in New York City but across the US as well. Racial inequality remains deeply entrenched, with millions of Black youth driven into longer-lasting unemployment. And all this was topped off in 1974–75 by capitalism's first worldwide slump in thirty-five years and the first extensive joblessness faced by workers in this country since before World War II.

The recovery from that downturn has been an extended one, but it has been shallow and uneven, with continuing high levels of unemployment despite an expansion of jobs. The official jobless rate during the recovery never dropped below levels that marked the worst points in the recessions of 1948, 1954, and 1970. Inflation is now back in the double digits again this year, and a new recession has begun.

Crisis of expectations

What is the cumulative effect of all this? It is changing the attitudes, expectations, and consciousness of American workers. Initially stunned by the suddenness and ferocity of the assault, workers are more and more ready to fight back.

The public response to each new capitalist breakdown or crisis is more skeptical than to a previous one. In regard to the current gas crisis, for example, fewer workers believe the propaganda that "the Arabs" are causing it. More and more working people hold the oil monopolies to blame. You can think of other examples.

Each new trial balloon by Washington about military intervention abroad, any threat of a new war, draws a bristling reaction.

The recent nationwide strike by independent truckers to win higher rates to offset skyrocketing diesel costs drew greater sympathy than previous actions. Although truckers didn't win their demands, the support they gained among union and nonunion workers—including many rank-and-file Teamsters—forced the Teamsters union officialdom to take a less openly hostile stance than before. It stood in contrast to the bureaucrats' open strikebreaking against independent steel haulers last year, working hand in glove with the steel bosses and FBI.[10]

Rail workers in Minnesota had a brilliant stroke when—as part of the campaign they're waging against the Milwaukee Road bankruptcy fraud—they put out a button and T-shirt with the simple slogan: "Investigate Milwaukeegate." That button is being worn up and down the Milwaukee line as a symbol of defiance of management. They didn't have to say another word to any worker. They just held up the word "Milwaukeegate," and it told the story.[11]

The rail workers love those buttons. The bosses and the government despise them.

∽

Five. Why is this happening? Why are we seeing these sprouts of class consciousness today? Is something more

---

10. See glossary: Independent truckers.

11. See glossary: Milwaukee Road and freight carriers' offensive.

"Independent truckers are organizing to win
higher rates to cover rising fuel and other costs."

THE MINNEAPOLIS STAR

Thursday, June 7, 1979   Copyright 1979 Minneapolis Star and Tribune Company   Single copy 20¢
A Section, Part 1

Angry drivers blockade truck stops

By GEORGE MONAGHAN
and DAVID E. EARLY
Minneapolis Star Staff Writers

Independent truckers, angered about rising diesel costs and the 55-mile-an-hour speed limit, blockaded truck stops in Minnesota today in what some said was the beginning of a nationwide strike.

State police today said most of the estimated 100 truck stops in Minnesota have been closed by the blockade.

Mandy Olson, president of the Minnesota Independent Truckers Association, said he knows of at least one truck stop that refused to close.

He said Stockman's Truck Stop in St. Paul, and High Forest Truck Stop in Rochester, Minn., had notified him they were closed.

Another truck stop, Ray's North Star, on U.S. Highway 12 near Afton, Minn., has been closed since Wednesday afternoon, according to its operator, Ray Casperson. Trucks were blocking the station from both sides early today as truckers slept in their cabs or drank coffee.

Ron Olson, assistant manager at Ray's, said about 15 trucks were

blocking pumps at the stop, normally open 24 hours.

At Stockmen's, about eight trucks were blocking pumps. An employee said the truck stop's restaurant would remain open all night, as usual.

A few truck stops in the state reported that no attempt was made by the independent truckers to close them.

The truckers, however, closed down several other truck stops in the Midwest and West and blocked

at least one major highway.

Truckers in Utah opened the show of force, closing down nine major truck stops well before midnight (Minneapolis time) deadline for the protest. Drivers in Oregon and North Dakota also

blocked diesel pumps.

At least 300 trucks blocked both eastbound and westbound lanes of the Tri-State Tollway in Indiana at the Burns Harbor interchange, 20 miles east of the Illinois-Indiana border, for several hours early to-

day. Police detoured traffic onto adjacent roads.

Between 10 and 20 truckers blocked entrances and exits to the

Truckers
Turn to Page 12A

A semi blocked gasoline and diesel pumps at Ray's North Star Truck Stop on U.S. Highway 12 near Afton, Minn., this morning   Star Photo by William Seaman

WILLIAM SEAMAN/MINNEAPOLIS STAR

ARNOLD WEISSBERG/MILITANT

Top: Afton, Minnesota, June 1979. Striking independent truckers shut down diesel fueling stations across the state.

Bottom: Auto parts workers at Hyatt Roller Bearing in New Jersey join 1979 nationwide protests over price gouging by energy barons.

"The civil rights and women's rights struggles changed social attitudes and relations among workers. They advanced class unity and consciousness that the battles against race and sex discrimination are working-class questions."

Top: 1968 strike by sanitation workers in Memphis, Tennessee. Action registered confidence and combativity gained by workers who are Black as battle to bring down Jim Crow segregation in South advanced.

Bottom: November 1971. Some 3,000 joined first national march on Washington demanding repeal of all laws limiting women's right to choose abortion.

involved than just the impact of the crisis and its effects?

Here we have to look at the changing structure and composition of the American working class, and at the social and political struggles originating outside the union movement that paved the way for today's battles.

Over the past quarter century, we have seen a rise of struggles by Blacks in this country, which has given an impulse to fights by Chicanos, by Puerto Ricans, and by women. These struggles preceded the current beginnings of working-class radicalization, but they are becoming intertwined.

The civil rights and women's rights struggles have brought permanent changes in social and political attitudes. They have improved the relationship of class forces, heightened the self-confidence of oppressed layers of the working class, and advanced consciousness within the entire working class of common *class* interests, which include combating race and sex discrimination. We saw the vanguard place and social weight of workers who are Black in transforming the American labor movement.

Changing composition of working class

The composition of the American working class is strikingly different than it was several decades ago. In the last nineteen years alone, the number of women in the workforce has shot up from 33 million to 42 million. Going back to the period just after World War II, the participation rate of women in the labor force has risen from 31 percent in 1948 to 51 percent today.

In 1973 the US government recorded only a handful of women working in underground coal mines. But picking up the cudgel of Title VII of the federal Civil Rights Act of 1964—a victory won in struggle and blood by battles for Black rights over the past quarter century—women, including members of the Socialist Workers Party, fought their way into the mines. There were nearly 2,000 women working in coal mines in September 1978, and more than 2,500 by spring 1979. And figures like these are still rising.[12]

These changes affect workers' political and social attitudes and the explosiveness of their reactions to the employers' antilabor offensive.

The first big test for both employers and workers came in 1977–78 when the capitalist class and its government targeted the United Mine Workers, aiming to cripple the power of this major industrial union. The miners, receiving solidarity throughout the labor movement, rebuffed the coal operators and Carter administration. Workers throughout the country discovered during the coal strike that the weak officialdom was not the union—the fighting miners were the union. We can point to many other examples, as the ruling class increasingly targets industrial workers and the industrial unions and pushes this decisive sector of our class toward the center stage of American politics.[13]

The attacks themselves make it increasingly clear that underneath all political developments, two classes confront each other—us and them, workers and capitalists. In order to chart a winning strategy for any oppressed layer in society or for any progressive social goal, it becomes

---

12. By 2019 there were more than 76 million women in the labor force, or 57 percent of adult women. (Women's participation rate peaked at more than 60 percent in early 2001 and has since declined to a level roughly the same as in the 1980s.) With the sharp decline in coal mining jobs (from some 240,000 coal miners in 1978 to 39,000 in 2015), the employment of women in the mines dropped to just over 1,100 in 2015. Despite the sharp reduction in mine jobs, more coal was dug in the US in 2018 than in 1979.

13. See glossary: Coal strike (1977–78).

more and more important to understand the social weight of these two contestants and the relationship of forces between them.

The main trends in the American working class today—under the combined impact of the worldwide capitalist profit drive, the social protest movements of the sixties and seventies, and the changes in the composition of the workforce—are not unexpected by the Socialist Workers Party. We meet these new developments with a cadre prepared both by our political conquests and practical political experience of the past decade and a half.

~

Six. There is deepening class polarization in the US. Politics is less and less seen by working people and others as simply the clash of good and bad, differing individual opinions, or even a conflict between a disembodied "right" and "left" detached from real class forces.

"The history of all hitherto existing society is the history of class struggles," Marx and Engels proclaimed in the opening paragraphs of the Communist Manifesto. That is the starting point of Marxism, historical materialism, and communism. All politics reflect the struggle of class against class.

Class against class
The growing consciousness of this fundamental fact of politics points out the road to resolving the problems of the oppressed and exploited. This is understood by relatively few workers today, but it will be by many more over the years. It points along the road of mobilizing the workers and our allies to fight for a workers and farmers government that can begin to take up the task of constructing a

society truly in the interests of humanity.

Social movements, such as the Black and Chicano movements, the women's liberation movement, and other progressive social protest struggles unfold in accord with their own dynamics of development, shaped by the broader class struggle and relationship of class forces. Their dynamics cannot be reduced to the laws of the struggle between capital and labor, let alone the laws that govern the fight to build a class-struggle left wing in the unions.

These social movements march to their own pace and rhythms and cannot be regimented to the schemas of the Stalinists, social democrats, and sectarians of all stripes. Understanding their specific dynamics, participating in these struggles, following their course of development, championing their progressive demands, is decisive in building a revolutionary workers party.

But as I just noted, these social movements are *not* independent from the relationship of forces established in the unfolding class struggle, nor from the state of confidence, class consciousness, and politicization of the vanguard of the working class.

To the contrary, the class struggle sets the political framework within which all social movements operate. It determines the form of their development and the prospects for their success or failure. At the same time, the class struggle itself is shaped, in part, by the course and outcome of these social movements. That's why we emphasize the interaction and interdependence of the struggles of the oppressed and the labor movement.

∼

Seven. As this class polarization deepens, a political polarization follows in its wake. The ruling class must *pro-*

pagandize to attempt to reverse the widespread antiwar attitudes among working people. It must *propagandize* to justify its takebacks and attacks on the working class and unions, Blacks, women, the handicapped, rebellious youth, and others. It tries to *explain away* its responsibility for catastrophes and breakdowns by putting the blame on the Arabs, "foreign imports," "unruly" unions, "welfare cheats," and other scapegoats.

Pressures on petty-bourgeois radicals

This concerted propaganda offensive puts tremendous pressure on the petty-bourgeois "intelligentsia," including the radicals among them. Witness the virtually universal condemnation in this milieu of Vietnam's intervention in Kampuchea (Cambodia) to help drive out the murderous Pol Pot regime; their collapse (à la Joan Baez) in face of Washington's campaign to isolate and punish Vietnam using the pretext of the "boat people" exodus since the victory and expropriation of capitalist property there since reunification in 1975.

Or the recent announcement by Paul Sweezy, the founding and decades-long editor of the "independent socialist" *Monthly Review*, before an audience of 1,000 in New York, that in light of this year's wars between Vietnam, Kampuchea, and China, Marxism no longer provides an adequate explanation of existing "postcapitalist" societies.[14]

These phenomena are symptomatic of the ideological pressures emanating from the ruling class. The middle-class intellectuals, in unison with the capitalist media, call it "a crisis of Marxism." It's actually a crisis facing all those who look for answers to great practical and theoretical problems confronting humanity somewhere else than by

---

14. See glossary: Vietnam; Cambodia.

starting with the interests of the international working class.

It's not a "crisis of Marxism." It's a crisis of petty-bourgeois politics.

The political disorientation in this quarter is different from the impact of the capitalist crisis on other petty-bourgeois social layers, especially on exploited sectors that are the weightiest potential allies of the working class, such as working farmers, craftspeople, owner-operators, and small proprietors. Intensifying struggles by the working class against big business and its political parties will divide the petty bourgeoisie and attract entire sections to the camp of the workers and oppressed. That will happen as they see the battalions of American labor move into action, providing decisive answers to the capitalist crisis, fighting for the interests of all toilers—a working-class program.

Until the American labor movement begins acting on a program of struggle that can attract allies in large numbers, this crisis of perspective among the petty-bourgeois intelligentsia and radicals will continue to deepen. The less they're connected with the working class and its basic institutions, the more they will be susceptible to self-absorption, reactionary mystical concepts, and pressures to subordinate everything else to "making it."

∼

Eight. These initial seven points lead to one simple and imperative political and organizational conclusion for communist workers: to get the great majority of our members and leaders into industry *now*—both *here* and *around the world.* That's the only way we can affect and be affected by these important changes in politics.

Regardless of the pace, the changes described here

will put their mark on the rest of the twentieth century and the opening of the twenty-first. Only by making this political turn to the industrial working class and unions can we position ourselves to meet the political responsibilities and take advantage of the opportunities we know are coming.

This is how we will develop a tested leadership, capable of regrouping with revolutionary currents in the workers movement – something we must do if we are to construct mass proletarian parties able to lead the workers to power, as well as to build a revolutionary international. Such currents will initially be drawn to us not because they know anything about our programmatic continuity with the Bolsheviks. They will be won by the attractive power of growing parties of socialist workers that have proven themselves as leaders in class combat and have shown the capacity *in action* to score victories in the interests of the toilers.

As the crisis of capitalism drives the toilers to fight back, other revolutionary currents *will* arise both in the semicolonial world, as well as in the labor movement and among workers and the oppressed in the advanced capitalist countries. We must be able to reach out to these fighters and link up with them, winning them to the course Lenin fought for. The course the Socialist Workers Party has always fought for. Only parties of industrial workers can exert that attractive power.

II.

How does our turn to industry advance our programmatic and strategic aims of transforming the labor movement into an instrument of class struggle, constructing a revolutionary proletarian party, and leading the working class and oppressed in establishing a workers and farmers government?

That's what the next eight points are about.

∽

Nine. What is our goal in the unions?

Quite simply, as Leon Trotsky explained in "Trade Unions In the Epoch of Imperialist Decay," our goal is to transform the American unions into "instruments of the revolutionary movement of the proletariat."[15]

What we do is aimed at moving toward trade unions that can become mass revolutionary organizations of combat for the American working class. In the process, we'll build the irreplaceable *political* instrument of our class—a mass proletarian party.

Fight to transform the unions

Our starting point is not confined to the economic functions of the unions, as basic and vital as those functions are. That's how class-collaborationist misleaders of labor want workers to see their unions—*at best.* By promoting that narrow conception, the bureaucrats are steadily weakening the capacity of the unions to defend the economic interests of their members and organize the unorganized.

Our starting point is the social character and political life that surround and dominate everything the unions do, including the gains they can win in the fight over wages, hours, and job conditions. We chart our strategic approach and judge our tactics in the labor movement by keeping

---

15. A draft article found on Trotsky's desk at the time of his assassination by an agent of Stalin in August 1940. It is published in *Tribunes of the People and the Trade Unions.*

our eyes fixed on the class-struggle leadership that can and will emerge from the ranks. That's where the future of the unions lies.

We don't begin with the unions as they seem right now, or as they were a few years ago. We chart our course in light of how the unions are changing, what they are becoming, and what they *must* become if they are to be able to fight and win. We give no guarantees about how many unions will be transformed into revolutionary instruments of struggle. We're not prophets but revolutionaries who work to steer developments in the direction of strengthening the unity of the working class in struggle.

One thing we do know. The socialist victory is inconceivable without the *struggle* to transform the unions into revolutionary instruments. And the construction of a revolutionary workers party is impossible without participating in that struggle.

As class battles unfold, there will be far-reaching changes in factories and working-class neighborhoods that spill beyond any organizational forms that currently exist, changes we can't foresee or imagine. Some organizations will be destroyed. Others will be transformed and revolutionized.

The fight itself is what is decisive in forging a revolutionary proletarian leadership.

～

Ten. What, then, do we have to do to move toward this goal of transforming the unions? What do we counterpose to the class-collaborationist perspective of the encrusted union bureaucracy, which holds back and saps the power of the American working-class movement? Against this class collaborationism—which is the bible of the current labor officialdom—socialist workers explain the need for, develop the program of, and seek to attract and educate the initial cadres of *a class-struggle left wing in the unions.*

Our elementary programmatic guidelines for this task are straightforward. We often sum them up this way:

• We fight for *union democracy* in all its forms, so the power of workers can be brought to bear.

• We fight for *solidarity* with other workers—organized and unorganized—and with struggles of all the oppressed and exploited here and around the world.

• We fight for *political independence* from the capitalist state and all its instruments. That includes the bourgeoisie's two-party system (and the occasional "third-party" spinoffs it inevitably generates).

Our industrial union fractions are learning how to combine three things to advance these programmatic goals:

1. Socialist propaganda: presenting our program through talking politics with co-workers; sales of the *Militant* and of books on working-class history and politics; and SWP election campaigns, forums, and classes.

2. Organizing, talking up, and involving co-workers, our unions, and workers and the labor movement as a whole in struggles around social and political issues—from helping defend women's health clinics that provide abortions and family planning, to supporting the Equal Rights Amendment for women.[16] From demanding the arrest and prosecution of cops responsible for brutality and killings of working people, to mobilizing workers and youth against rightist groups that aim to block school or housing desegregation. From solidarity with the Nicaraguan, Grenada, and Cuban revolutions, to supporting the fight against the white supremacist regime in South Africa and defending the framed-up and imprisoned revolutionists in Iran.

3. Taking part in struggles around wages, working con-

---

16. See glossary: Equal Rights Amendment.

"Socialist workers involve others in solidarity with the Nicaraguan, Grenada, and Cuban revolutions, against apartheid in South Africa, and in defense of imprisoned revolutionists in Iran."

SEPTEMBER 7, 1979   50 CENTS   VOLUME 43/NUMBER 34

THE MILITANT

A SOCIALIST NEWSWEEKLY/PUBLISHED IN THE INTERESTS OF THE WORKING PEOPLE

International outcry demands:

STOP EXECUTION OF SOCIALISTS IN IRAN!

By David Frankel

AUGUST 29—Sentences of death were handed down by a secret tribunal in Ahvaz, Iran, against twelve imprisoned members of the Iranian Socialist Workers Party (HKS) on August 26. An international outcry and protests within Iran have blocked the immediate execution of the twelve, but they remain in the gravest danger. Emergency protests from around the world are vital to saving their lives.

None of the twelve socialists condemned to death, nor two others condemned to life imprisonment on August 25, have committed any crime.

All of them were tried in secret by the government's Special Court in Ahvaz. They were denied any legal representation, the right to call witnesses in their behalf, and even the right to speak in their own defense.

Sentenced to death are: Hadi Adib, Hormoz Fallahi,

Firooz Farzinpoor, Morteza Gorgzadeh, Mostafa Gorgzadeh, Ali Hashemi, Kambiz Lajavardi, Mahmoud Kafaie, Kia Mahdavi, Mohammed Pourkahvaz, Mostafa Seifazadi, and Hamid Shahrabi.

Two women HKS members received life sentences— Fatima Fallahi and Mahsa Hashemi.

A dispatch from the government's Pars News Agency, published in the Au-

gust 26 issue of the Tehran daily Bamedad, listed the following charges against Fallahi and Hashemi:

Participation in anti-Islamic and anti-popular activities.

Agitation against the central government.

Criticism of the central government for being undemocratic.

Instigation of riot.

Responsibility for the

"tragedy in Naqadeh" (one of the earliest clashes in which the army of the central government was sent in against the Kurdish population).

Having praised the "antirevolutionary Kurdish people."

Encouraging the armed struggle of the Kurdish people against the central government.

Continued on page 4

Nicaraguan leaders appeal for international aid

Eyewitness report: gov't attacks profiteers
—PAGES 8-10

Above: September 7, 1979, *Militant* backs world campaign to free 12 members of Socialist Workers Party (HKS) of Iran sentenced to death, and 2 others to life terms, in oil-rich Khuzistan province. Their "crime" was popularizing socialist views among workers in oilfields, refineries, steel mills, and other workplaces and oppressed communities. By April 1980, international effort had won freedom for all 14. **Left:** Fatima Fallahi and Mahsa Hashemi as they are released from prison.

"In face of capitalists' cutthroat drive for profits, wrote Marx and Engels in 1847, workers 'club together to keep up the rate of wages' and defend job conditions. Inevitably, they 'begin to form combinations (trade unions)' against the employing class."

Garment workers in San Francisco demand unpaid back wages from bosses, October 1992.

VED DOOKHUN/MILITANT

ditions, speedup, and safety that incessantly develop on the job and will increase as the bosses step up their anti-labor offensive.

A periphery on the job, in the unions

We can't look at our work in the unions solely as preparing for a class-struggle left wing—which as yet has no organizational form—and in the process directly recruiting workers to the party. That oversimplifies matters. Because as we carry out this course, something else begins to happen—something that will be an important gauge of the work of our industrial fractions. That's the growth of our periphery on the job and in the labor movement.

The party will attract layers of workers—tens to begin with, then hundreds, and later thousands. They may not join the party right away. But they will follow our press, read books by party leaders, go with us to a conference or demonstration, introduce us to their friends and families, support our election campaigns, attend some of our forums, be influenced by our members, and become better acquainted with our ideas. They will look to the SWP as an identifiable and alternative political pole. They will start picking up elements of our Marxist program.

Our capacity to draw around us such a layer of workers will be an essential ingredient of forging a class-struggle left wing as well as building the party. It's a key conquest of the small but growing number of steady *Militant* readers and subscribers our fractions are developing among co-workers.

This is nothing new in the revolutionary working-class movement. It's been true ever since the British industrial bourgeoisie tried to crush the spirit of those they forcibly turned into the first proletarians. There has always been a layer of workers who resisted, who were inclined toward fighting for their own class interests by any means necessary, toward revolutionary action, and toward looking for a program to help them move forward.

That is what Marxism really is, as Marx and Engels explained from the very inception of the communist movement. It's not a set of ideas. It's simply the generalization of the lessons of our victories and defeats. It expresses the interests of our class—the ideas vanguard workers are looking for, the program they need in order to win.[17] We want to attract those rebels in the plants, mines, and mills, get them involved in *working-class action*, and recruit the best of them to the SWP.

~

Eleven. What will a class-struggle left wing look like? Do we have a model to go by? I've often been asked that.

The honest answer is that we don't know. We have no preview of the form a class-struggle left wing is likely to take in the American labor movement.

We do know the prospects are advanced by the emergence of fighters in specific struggles around union democracy and class solidarity. We know the process will almost surely be interconnected with hard-fought class battles in which the leadership of certain union structures—committees, locals, districts—will be won. But we can't foresee the process, and there's no point in speculating.

Lessons to read, study, absorb

Nonetheless, there's one educational example in American labor history of significant motion toward a class-struggle left wing and the development of a revolutionary union

---

17. See the final item in this book, "Communism Is Not a Doctrine but a Movement," page 177.

leadership. That's the leadership of what became Minneapolis Teamsters Local 544 in the 1930s and the Midwest organizing drive spearheaded by it. This experience gives us a great advantage, since our party led Local 544. One of its central leaders—Farrell Dobbs—wrote a detailed record of what happened and its lessons for us and other vanguard workers to read, study, and absorb.

Those four books—*Teamster Rebellion, Teamster Power, Teamster Politics,* and *Teamster Bureaucracy*—are worth reading, rereading, and reviewing every year. The more comrades get into industry, get to know the unions, and begin operating as part of party fractions, the more we'll get out of those books every time we go back to them. Each time we'll find something new and richer than we remembered.

Of all the periods of significant trade union work by our party, this one is the most useful for us today.

More so than the period right before US imperialism's entry into World War II. While the party at that time, from 1939 through 1941, had made a proletarian turn, we had to operate under severe restraints and with great caution due to Washington's crackdown on labor militants, as President Franklin Roosevelt prepared to drag the toiling classes of America into that imperialist slaughter to defend the interests of his property-owning class. The federal indictment and conviction of our leading comrades in 1941, with the cooperation of the top Teamster officialdom, occurred in this period.[18] As a result, our trade union work was marked by a mode of functioning different from what the party faces today.

The Teamster experience in the mid-1930s is also more directly relevant now than the party's union activity af-

---

18. See glossary: Smith Act trial (1941).

ter the end of the brief postwar labor upsurge. Our trade union fractions from mid-1947 through the early 1950s—in maritime, auto, steel, and other industries—did valuable work. But these years, too, were marked by conditions very different from those we now face. The American labor movement was in retreat, despite sporadic fights.

As the US rulers pursued the Cold War and witch-hunt, we had to put a great deal of effort into tactical maneuvers to buy time and hold off attempts to drive class-struggle militants out of the unions. We sometimes supported this or that lesser-evil caucus or candidate for a union post, just to have space to function. We sought to maintain a number of cadres in the unions in preparation for any possible up-surge—which, as it turned out, did not come for a couple of decades.

The Teamster experience from 1934 through 1938 trans-pired during years of deep capitalist crisis and growing working-class militancy and radicalization. An entire gen-eration of rank-and-file workers were beginning to look for a way forward. By 1934 a mass labor upsurge was in the offing—whether it would come then, a year later, or three or five years was not important. There was a mounting de-sire to fight back and growing capacity to do so.

This is the period—its rise and fall—that Farrell recounts in the four Teamster books.

The Minneapolis branch consciously colonized the trucking industry. Farrell explains that party leaders care-fully thought this out. Given the agriculture and milling in the area, they considered trucking the decisive industry in Minneapolis. Fortunately, our members could also get into this sector and build a party fraction. So that's what we did.

The branch leaders in Minneapolis were looking for young workers beginning to radicalize and willing to fight. They were open to the possibility that even a relatively young worker who had voted for Herbert Hoover for president in November 1932 might be leading militant working-class struggles only a year or so later. That's what happened with Farrell Dobbs. He voted Republican a little more than a year before he helped lead some of the greatest battles in the history of the American working class.

The Minneapolis socialists understood and valued what many others saw as obstacles—the inexperience and rawness of young workers, for example. That meant the ranks didn't have to unlearn so many things, Farrell points out. They hadn't been brainwashed to believe that a layer of labor bureaucrats was more militant and "progressive" than they were.

Once these young workers went into action, they learned fast. True, it took a series of blows from the employers before they looked to their union, and some further blows before they looked beyond their initial union leaders.

None of our party cadres in Minneapolis began as elected leaders of General Drivers Local 574 (later Local 544). Not a single one held an official post throughout the coal yard strike in early 1934 and the first of the big strike battles later that year.

With the approval of Teamster union officials, we began by working with other rank-and-file militants to set up the unofficial strike committee. Only after the second strike, in the summer of 1934, did the rank and file demand that the tested leaders of that battle be elected to the top union posts.

The workers ran up against a lot of former officials who got in their way. But they also found a couple of officials— Bill Brown was one of them—who were changed by these experiences, came over, and helped lead the fight. As Farrell explains, we did not find, and never would have found,

"There's one example in US labor history of motion toward a class-struggle left wing. That's Minneapolis Teamsters Local 544 and the Midwest organizing drive in the 1930s."

MINNESOTA HISTORICAL SOCIETY

Through hard-fought strikes, workers in trucking made Minneapolis a union town. *Top:* May 1934. Mass pickets were central to victory, ensuring no trucks could move in market area.

Bottom: Teamster strike leaders (from left) Bill Brown, Farrell Dobbs, and Carl Skoglund. Dobbs, a central leader of these battles, was national secretary of the Socialist Workers Party from 1953 to 1972.

Inset: Front page of Teamster paper, August 22, 1934.

Milestone on the Road to Peace!

THEREFORE BE IT RESOLVED

THAT.... FIFTY THOUSAND TRADE UNIONISTS, DECLARES IT'S UNALTERABLE OPPOSITION TO ALL WAR PREPARATIONS AND....IT'S FIRM OPPOSITION TO ANY WAR LAUNCHED BY THE GOVERNMENT;

THAT WE SHALL JOIN WITH ALL OTHER FORCES IN THE LABOR MOVEMENT WHO SHARE OUR VIEWS FOR THE PURPOSE OF CONSOLIDATING THE STRONGEST POSSIBLE MOVEMENT OF RESISTANCE TO WAR AND TO THE WAR-MONGERS

RESOLUTION ADOPTED BY MINN. CENTRAL LABOR UNION

Carlo

CARLO/NORTHWEST ORGANIZER, APRIL 14, 1938

Top: Omaha, Nebraska, June 1937. Strikers celebrate in front of first truck to move after winning union contract from Arrow Motors Freight. Victory was part of drive, led by the Minneapolis Teamsters, that within a few years organized a quarter million over-the-road truckers in 11 states.

Bottom: April 1938 *Northwest Organizer* reports resolution opposing Washington's war drive adopted by Minneapolis unions representing 50,000 workers. Local 544 leaders mobilized labor opposition to US imperialism's aims.

Bill Brown by looking for *him*. Instead, by organizing and mobilizing *the ranks*, we bumped into Bill Brown along the way.

Once this new Teamster leadership got rolling, it practiced the kind of class-struggle politics we've been discussing. It was the most democratic union in US history, controlled by the ranks. It practiced solidarity with the unemployed, the unorganized, independent truck owner-operators, many local unions, and working farmers in the Minneapolis–St. Paul area. The Teamsters acted on the knowledge that solidarity was not only part and parcel of advancing the overall struggle, but also the only way to defend and build their own union.

From the beginning, these revolutionary union leaders charted a course toward building a labor party. They didn't wait until a class-struggle left wing was formed to advance this perspective. The existence of the Farmer-Labor Party in Minnesota, and the illusions many workers had in it, posed more sharply and immediately than elsewhere in the US the need for a labor party based on the unions, independent of the bosses' state and political parties. Our cadres leading Local 544 oriented toward winning the FLP's ranks to a class-struggle program.

Local 544 leaders mobilized the ranks to use union power. Its members used every sort of flanking tactic and tactical nuance that comrades are beginning to get some acquaintance with today. These Teamster leaders fought politically against government frame-ups of union militants and mobilized labor opposition to the coming imperialist world war.

In doing all this, these revolutionary union leaders developed not only the nucleus of a class-struggle left wing and a growing layer of union cadres around it. They also brought around them a periphery of workers who read our press more or less regularly, and absorbed more and more of our working-class program. Party cadres in the over-the-road organizing campaign launched a few years later recruited new members all the way from Dallas to Cincinnati, from Oklahoma City to Louisville to Detroit—nuclei of truck drivers and other workers who were members of our party.

Thinking workers discovered the need for a revolutionary party in combat situations—revolutionary centralism, political homogeneity, internal democracy, and a solid proletarian composition.

So, although there's no model of a nationwide class-struggle left wing in the labor movement, at least we're fortunate to have had an experience where leaders of the communist movement consistently applied our program and methods in a period of rising labor struggles.

Even here, as Farrell cautions in the Teamster series, we'll find no tactical guide. The books project a strategic framework and give a concrete account of rich class-struggle experiences that may have similarities to situations we'll confront. But we won't derive a single tactical formula out of these books—or out of *any* book. Such moves will be worked out by the comrades and co-workers involved in the particular situation on the basis of the circumstance they confront.

~

Twelve. The deepening crisis of capitalism more and more drives home the importance of the method of the document we often refer to as the Transitional Program. It's one of our most fundamental programmatic documents.[19]

---

19. The party in the United States today called the Socialist Workers Party was founded in 1919 as the Communist Party and celebrated its hundredth anniversary as this book was being published. That year marked

At a time when world capitalism was plunging humanity toward the second world interimperialist slaughter,
Trotsky pinpointed the key obstacle to the progress of
socialist revolution under those conditions, which he described as "a prerevolutionary period of agitation, propaganda and organization"—very different from the situation the working class and our allies confront in the
United States or a big majority of the world today.

The SWP's 1938 program is not a tactical handbook, hov-
ering above time and objective conditions. It provides the
strategic framework for communist political work. Above
all, we must absorb and be able to use its method in responding to fresh events that continually come up, the new
combinations of circumstances that no one can foresee.

First, Trotsky said, revolutionists act in ways that give
workers and the oppressed more confidence in ourselves
and in our capacity to struggle—ways that inspire and
convince working people that we *can* affect politics and
change the world. That's the opposite of what workers
have been taught about ourselves by all the institutions of
capitalist society.

We seek to convince our class that we can transform
society by fighting together, fighting uncompromisingly—
and by fighting intelligently, seriously. In the course of
day-to-day battles, we seek to convince workers there is a
way to emancipate ourselves and all our allies, and that our

---

the founding of the Communist International, led by V.I. Lenin and the
Bolshevik Party in Soviet Russia. Drawing on the program and strategy
of that world organization, Leon Trotsky collaborated with the Socialist
Workers Party leadership in 1938, on the eve of World War II, in drafting what became both the SWP's basic programmatic document and the
program of the world movement the SWP helped lead at that time, the
Fourth International. It is published in the book *The Transitional Program for Socialist Revolution* (Pathfinder, 1977).

class alone can bring it about.

"All methods are good which raise the class consciousness of the workers, their trust in their own forces, their readiness for self-sacrifice in the struggle," as Trotsky put it toward the end of the Transitional Program.

"The impermissible methods," he said, "are those which implant fear and submissiveness in the oppressed in the face of their oppressors, which crush the spirit of protest and indignation or substitute for the will of the masses—the will of the leaders; for conviction—compulsion; for an analysis of reality—demagogy and frame-up."[20]

This spirit of combative class independence will be crowned by the formation and federation of what in Russia were known as soviets, the Russian word for councils. That is, mass workers organizations that will lead the fight for power and, after victory, will become the organizational bedrock on which to begin the socialist reconstruction of society.

Second, we act as worker-revolutionaries. As Trotsky explained in *In Defense of Marxism,* and James P. Cannon in *The Struggle for a Proletarian Party*, workers are subject to the coercion of real conditions of life. We know in our bones that we live in an imperfect world—one we want to improve and change. We treasure every advance. We fight to preserve every inch of conquered territory. We don't begin with schemas. We don't check whether or not reality measures up to some predetermined model—and, if it doesn't, retreat to the sidelines to await a better day.

Workers start from our current points of support and try to move forward from there, using the weapons we have at hand. Our course of action seeks to build bridges from the problems workers face, and their current under-

---

20. Trotsky, *The Transitional Program*, p. 192 [2019 printing].

standing of those problems, to broader socialist solutions.

This brings us to the third crucial underpinning of the 1938 program—and its starting point. The goal is for the consciousness of workers to be changed through the experiences and struggles in which we are engaged. We start from the *objective* economic and political situation—the needs of the class and the developing contradictions of the capitalist system on a world scale, not the state of mind of most workers at any given moment.

The job of the program, Trotsky said in discussions with leaders of the Socialist Workers Party, is "to find the connecting links and lead the masses" from fights for the most basic democratic and immediate demands, including trade union demands, to a course for "the revolutionary conquest of power." It is our duty to make "this gap between objective and subjective factors as short as possible," he said.[21]

Communist workers have to explain the truth, while doing so in a way that makes our program most accessible and understandable to workers. That's a task we encounter every day on the job. It's one that our candidates grapple with, and that we constantly try to improve on in the *Militant*.

Finally, Trotsky said, "Naturally, if I close my eyes I can write a good rosy program that everybody will accept. But it will not correspond to the situation, and the program must correspond to the situation." The decay of capitalism itself, Trotsky assured us, is the paramount factor in bridg-

---

21. Trotsky, *The Transitional Program*, p. 133. In late 1937 Trotsky requested that an SWP leadership delegation visit him in Mexico, where he was living in exile, for discussions that would aid him in drafting the program. In March 1938 three party leaders did so, James P. Cannon, Max Shachtman, and Vincent R. Dunne. Transcripts of those exchanges, as well as discussions organized later that year, are published in *The Transitional Program for Socialist Revolution*. Several are also available in *Tribunes of the People and the Trade Unions*.

ing the gap between objective reality and workers' current consciousness. "Under the blows of the objective crisis, the millions of unemployed," he said, this consciousness can change rapidly.[22]

This, then, brings us to the problem of how to present our demands, how to explain our slogans so we can do our utmost to close the gap.

∿

Thirteen. Nineteen eighty is a presidential election year. This provides us with a special platform to explain our program. As long as the capitalists keep holding presidential elections every four years, we'll keep on using them to present a socialist alternative to American workers.

Campaigning for our program

What will be the central issues of the 1980 campaign? Many are already clear.

We'll be campaigning against Washington's war threats targeting Nicaragua, Grenada, and Cuba.

We'll be demanding a shorter workweek with no cut in pay, as well as an escalator clause for wages and government benefits, as an answer to the double whammy of unemployment and double-digit inflation.

We'll be pointing to the need to nationalize the energy trust, the Milwaukee Road rail carrier, Chrysler, and other industries that are raising such havoc for millions of working people and our families in face of skyrocketing gasoline and heating oil prices, as well as massive layoffs and attacks on safety conditions on the job.

We'll be supporting strikes and other labor battles, including efforts to organize the unorganized and fights

---

22. Trotsky, *The Transitional Program*, p. 204.

around union democracy such as those we've been part of in the USWA and UTU in recent years.

Our candidates and campaigns will be mobilizing solidarity in action with all kinds of local and national struggles to advance the rights and conditions of Blacks, Chicanos, Native Americans, and women. These include fights against racist violence and police brutality we've been involved in—from Detroit to Decatur, Alabama, and Tupelo, Mississippi—as well as for ratification the Equal Rights Amendment and defense of a woman's right to choose abortion.

The presidential campaign offers the broadest opportunity for the Socialist Workers Party to explain the need for American labor to break with the capitalist two-party system—with the Democrats and Republicans—and launch a labor party based on the unions.

Comrades in the industrial fractions confirm that our ability to get a hearing among working people on the need for a break with the bosses' political parties is increasing. Given the current stage of the class struggle, the slogan of a labor party right now is not an agitational campaign in the working class and labor movement, but an important part of our election propaganda. It's one of the ways we explain to fellow workers our alternative to the bankruptcy of the two-party system and the labor bureaucracy's dead-end reliance on the Democratic Party.

Workers who are most open to the need to break from the employers' state and from their political parties today will be attracted to the SWP election campaigns and to the Socialist Workers Party. Over the next eighteen months, Andrew Pulley and Matilde Zimmermann, our candidates for president and vice-president, will be talking to working people about all these pressing national and international political issues before our class. And they'll be urging workers who agree with them to support the SWP campaign, to subscribe to the *Militant,* and to join the SWP and YSA.

～

Fourteen. The end point of what we call labor's strategic line of march—the goal of all our work and all the struggles of our class—is a workers and farmers government. From Marx and Engels through Lenin and Trotsky, this has been the goal sought after through the mass revolutionary action of the working class and our allies. In the words of the SWP Constitution, "to educate and organize the working class in order to establish a workers and farmers government, which will abolish capitalism in the United States and join in the worldwide struggle for socialism."

This underlines the importance of the interplay between the unions and social protest movements. We don't call on oppressed layers of the population to wait on the unions before they organize and start fighting—they never have and never should.

The more unions move toward becoming revolutionary organizations of class combat, however, the more union power will be used to fight around social and political issues on behalf of all labor's allies. Mass workers mobilizations will grow more powerful, and proletarian leaders will come to the fore in all social struggles. That's what we fight for.

～

Fifteen. We have also begun to recognize the strategic importance of correctly gauging the social weight and political centrality of various struggles and issues. This is essential to the allocation of our forces and the establishment of political priorities.

> **"Trade unions must organize the unorganized and look carefully after the interests of the worst-paid trades, such as agricultural laborers."**
>
> **Karl Marx, 1866**

MATT HERRESHOFF/MILITANT

SAM BRASCH

Top: Yakima Valley, Washington, April 1987. Members of farm workers union on strike for a contract at Pyramid apple orchards. Sign says in part, "The union benefits us all." Farm laborers are "the brothers-in-arms" of other workers, "two parts of one and the same class," says the 1938 program of the Socialist Workers Party.

Bottom: Small farmers, though a different class from workers, are strategic allies in common fight for a workers and farmers government. Squeezed between rising production costs and falling prices for their produce, they are being driven off the land. In photo, February 1979, 3,000 farmers roll into Washington, DC, demanding crop price supports.

We champion all progressive struggles. But key to transforming American labor is our understanding that the oppressed Black nationality, working farmers, and women are the central strategic allies in the fight for a workers and farmers government.

Only acting in accordance with that judgment can the working class exert the maximum leverage in changing the relationship of class forces to our advantage and to the advantage of all our allies.

~

Sixteen. What do we mean by class consciousness?

It means looking at all social and political questions in class terms, not as individuals. To think primarily not about *me* but about *we*—about the class we are part of.

There's no way of turning a worker or anyone else who thinks only in individual terms into a proletarian revolutionist. Thinking of what you can accomplish *as part of a class* and *what your class can accomplish*—that is the jumping-off point of class consciousness.

'We' rather than 'me'

That may start with experiences that make personal solutions look less realistic and more difficult. Workers discover that other working people face the same difficulties they do—and are asking for help, offering solidarity, and showing a way to fight together.

Something else happens when you begin to think as *we* rather than *me*. You begin understanding there is another *we*. There is a *we* who in reality are a *they*—the capitalist ruling class. *They* are the class enemy of our class. Any policy based on collaboration with that enemy weakens *us* because it strengthens *them*.

Racism, race-baiting, sexism, protectionism, imperialist nationalism, "Buy America," making sacrifices for "our" company or "our" industry, supporting Washington's wars, you name it—all of them weaken our common fight as a class. All of them strengthen the enemy and shift the relationship of class forces further to our detriment. Acting in politics as part of this reactionary "we" hobbles our unions, lowers our wages, worsens our working conditions, and threatens our posterity and ultimately even our own lives.

With this understanding, we wage a *political* battle against those in our class—usually the relatively better-off, those hoping to escape their proletarian condition— who are the most susceptible to supporting the class-collaborationist misleaders of the labor movement and their reformist notions.

That was shown once again in the recent victory in the *Weber* case, when the US Supreme Court in June 1979 turned down Brian Weber's lawsuit seeking to overturn a key part of the contract negotiated by the United Steelworkers union at the Kaiser Aluminum plant in Gramercy, Louisiana.

Weber claimed he'd been a victim of "reverse discrimination" in the plant, and his suit had been upheld in lower courts. The Supreme Court rejected his effort to eliminate the job-training quota won under the USWA contract reserving half the trainee spots for Blacks and women. Prior to that new contract, while some 40 percent of workers at Gramercy were African American, less than 2 percent of the so-called skilled jobs—yes, not even 1 out of every 50!—had been held by workers who are Black. And *none* by women.

The battle that overturned the lower court's *Weber* decision was a victory not only for Blacks, Latinos, and women, but for American labor. The changes in consciousness in the working class brought about by the accomplishments of the Black struggle helped make this victory possible.

Opponents of equality for Blacks and women often argue that seniority must not be tampered with as a way of correcting discriminatory layoffs or job upgrading. But the USWA's 1974 consent decree with the basic steel companies strengthened the entire labor movement. It said that at least 50 percent of new hires would be Blacks and women, making it possible for them to bid on (and get training for) jobs in better-paying departments without losing their seniority in the plant.

This shows that something new is happening in the labor movement. And the fact that it happened in Gramercy, Louisiana, shows that the ruling class can't even find a secure refuge in the right-to-work-for-less South any more, or in the so-called Sun Belt. Those are no longer safe territory for the employers. The mighty struggles that defeated Jim Crow, combined with national and world events of the last decade, have provided tremendous impetus to the class struggle in the South, making it a key factor in American politics today.

Along with the big USWA organizing drive in Newport News—the biggest Southern organizing effort in nearly a quarter century—there was an important victory for workers at the big new GM plant in Oklahoma City.[23]

I was sitting with a cup of tea at about 7:00 a.m., watching CBS television news the morning after those workers in Oklahoma had voted 2–1 for the UAW. The reporters first interviewed GM management, who said they had honestly thought there had been no chance of the union winning. They said they were very surprised. After all, many workers had told them they didn't want a union! Obviously

---

23. See glossary: Steelworkers Local 8888 (Newport News, Virginia); Oklahoma City UAW organizing drive.

something had gone seriously wrong, the bosses said.

Then CBS interviewed a few workers who represented GM's company union. They just mumbled and tried to get off camera. But finally there was film of the celebration by the majority—the workers who had won, white and Black, young and old. It was a broad, militant, and proud rally.

These changes among American workers open up new vistas for the social struggles ahead.

III.

We've made significant progress in carrying out the turn this past year. We've learned quite a bit.

What, then, are the next steps in building our industrial union fractions? How do we proceed both on the political and organizational level in completing the turn, and conducting more and more of our activity through those fractions?

Building our industrial fractions
The concluding nine points address these important questions.

∽

Seventeen. Since the February 1978 meeting of the National Committee, we've said that our goal is to get a large majority of the party into industry and the industrial unions.

At the beginning of the turn a year and a half ago, the National Committee to some degree underestimated the party and its cadres. Consciously or unconsciously, we assumed there was a layer of comrades who—for various unstated reasons—should not go into industry. We also assumed there would be a layer who would personally not want to do what we've all been waiting for.

This turned out to be false. The lesson we have learned, the lesson the party has taught us in fewer than eighteen months, is a lesson for our entire world movement. When the membership and leadership are politically convinced of the opportunities for work as part of our class, layer after layer of comrades respond and do what's necessary to get an industrial job.

Comrades have organized their lives so they can be part of implementing the party's course. They've been helped by their branch committees and local leadership bodies working together. All kinds of seeming obstacles—this or that health problem, this or that time for adjustment—are overcome both through personal commitment and political leadership.

There are no broad categories of exceptions. Our turn is a general policy, and it *has* to be in order to be carried out to the end. We have former lawyers, doctors, dentists, professors, members of the building trades, teachers, and all varieties of public employees who are either already in industry or looking. Members of the National Committee, the Political Committee, staff writers, and editors have all been released from other assignments to be part of the turn. Over time there will be turnover, as comrades in industry are asked to take on full-time party assignments and vice versa.

The turn is universal. Everyone who is not in industry, and becomes convinced and finds it possible to get an industrial job, is welcome. We'll help you get in.

There's no "balance" whatsoever to our turn. We are putting all our eggs in one basket. Because that is the only way to build the nucleus of a proletarian party, the biggest industrial fractions, the most effective participation in the mass movement and in struggles of all kinds. It is the way to ensure the party the greatest political influence over time.

This is a deliberately and thoroughly unbalanced tactic—and it must be carried out that way. Or it won't work.

This is not because we think we know where the next big social and political explosions will take place, or how many, or at what exact tempo, or in which order. We don't. All we know is that such explosions *will* take place, and when they do, industrial workers will respond. In doing so, they will strengthen the fight to transform their unions—and themselves—in order to advance every struggle of the oppressed and exploited.

Our turn is the best way to ensure we will be part of these battles, that we will be in a position to advance our program and develop class-struggle leadership, and that a revolutionary party will be constructed and strengthened all along the way.

～

Eighteen. We carry out our activity in industry as we do everywhere else—as party work.

As part of an industrial fraction, we learn to function in a more disciplined way. We're discovering that comrades' self-confidence gets a boost, as does overall interest in politics and understanding of Marxism. As an industrial worker, it's easier to grasp Marxism as the generalized interests and line of march of a class.

Comrades discover a new way of reading, fresh insights we missed the first time around. Comrades who didn't think they would ever write for the *Militant* are becoming worker-correspondents.

～

Nineteen. Our goal is to get into the big plants, the big mines, the big mills, the big rail yards. We want to be in position to work with and influence the largest possible numbers of industrial workers in sizable workplaces and union locals.

A nationwide party

But we're also building a *nationwide* party. The United States has no Petrograd. Our class is spread throughout the country, in cities large and small and with different regional political and social characteristics. Only a nationwide party carrying out political activity in cities, towns, and rural areas can be involved in, keep in touch with, and help generalize the experiences of the American working class.

There are hundreds of areas in this country—much of the Upper Midwest, the Tidewater region of Virginia, the Piedmont region in North Carolina—with no gigantic cities but with large proletarian concentrations in basic industry and other workplaces. Sometimes these workers are unorganized, sometimes highly unionized.

Cities such as Miami, Washington, D.C., San Antonio, and Albuquerque are important political centers of this country, despite their *relatively* smaller concentrations of industrial workers. There is a large and important working-class Cuban community in Miami, and sizable Central American communities in both Miami and Washington, D.C. Given the changing attitudes toward the Cuban Revolution among Cubans in this country and the developing struggles in Central America, it is important to have branches in these cities for these reasons if no other—and there are plenty of others.

Not only Houston and Dallas, but San Antonio, Phoenix, and Albuquerque are centers of the Chicano population, as are Salt Lake City and Denver. Chicanos make up a substantial section of the industrial workforce in these cities, and there are many undocumented Mexican immigrant workers, as well.

Our party cannot afford to ignore the politics of these cities, or to lapse into illusions that we can "wait until later" to begin participating in the political life of all but the largest US industrial centers.

There is another misconception I've sometimes heard— that New York City and San Francisco are petty-bourgeois cities, not very important for a proletarian party. That's nonsense. These are major political centers of this country, each with a large working class and labor movement. If we can't have a functioning unit with a well-stocked bookstore and attractive public headquarters in New York and San Francisco, then we're doing something wrong.

Comrades have been ready to turn away from better-paying jobs to move to the unorganized Sun Belt, to go to the Piedmont, to go where more poorly paid and less unionized workers live and work. With somewhat less than a quarter of the workforce in unions right now, the conditions in places such as these are representative of those facing a majority of the American working class.[24]

$\sim$

Twenty. Leon Trotsky and Jim Cannon laid down two basic guidelines that our fractions are finding to be good starting points:

- Trotsky explained the need for workers to think socially and act politically.
- Cannon urged us to talk socialism.

The more progress we make in our turn, the more we've

---

24. Forty years later, in 2019, some 10.5 percent of workers in the US are organized. Some 6.4 percent of workers hired by private employers are in unions. This sharp and unrelenting decline is, above all, the product of the union officialdom's class-collaborationist course, which hamstrings the ranks and has seriously weakened the union movement.

found that these are the best guides for our fractions in industry. We're making the turn precisely because of the growing politicization and radicalization of sections of the working class. The combination of what is happening to workers on the job and what they see happening to them in capitalist society as a whole causes them to be more interested in politics, and to turn to their unions to fight. Their consciousness is being transformed.

We want the *Militant* to be known on the job. We've made progress on this. Socialist workers are selling the paper on the job and at the gates during other shifts.

It's through the *Militant,* as well as the books we publish and distribute, that our co-workers get to know who we are when fights break out around one issue or another.

We're supporters of Black rights and women's equality.

We're the people who are defending the Nicaraguan Revolution, the Grenada Revolution, the Cuban Revolution.

We're the workers who think there should be a shorter workweek with no cut in pay, workers' control of safety and production in the mines and factories, and that the unions must never subordinate the interests of the working class to the bosses' political parties and their government.

Comrades are discovering that being an SWP candidate is one of the very best ways of introducing ourselves and our ideas on the job. We urge our co-workers to become supporters of socialist candidates.

Our comrades can take part in the contest of stickers and T-shirts that goes on in the plants. We can plaster Pulley and Zimmermann slogans all over our work clothes. We can pin a Pulley button next to our Milwaukeegate button.

At the steel fraction meeting a few days ago, a comrade working at Sparrows Point in Baltimore said he has a co-worker whose hard hat says "Vote Socialist Workers" on the right and "Jesus Saves" on the left. That's great! We can work together to reach a workers and farmers government even before the Second Coming.

Young workers are both imaginative and defiant. A glimpse of this came up at the fraction meeting of party members in the International Association of Machinists, the IAM. In May the engine fell off a DC-10 just after take-off in Chicago, leading to a crash in which more than 270 people were killed. McDonnell Douglas went on a big propaganda blitz to whitewash the safety of the DC-10 and bolster the company's stock price. A comrade at the IAM fraction meeting said that when the company handed out T-shirts to employees with a picture of the DC-10, one worker took a pair of scissors, cut out one of the engines, and wore the shirt to work.

Next year this whole country is going to discuss which of the rotten gangs—those of Carter, Kennedy, or some Republican—is going to run the White House. We have a working-class alternative, a Socialist Workers Party alternative. This is how we're going to be operating in the factories.

❧

Twenty-one. There was some give-and-take in the party's discussion bulletin around whether or not comrades should seek out or accept union office. Two different questions sometimes get confused.

Socialists in the unions, of course, seek to be leaders and to take *leadership responsibility.* But this is *not* the same thing as taking union posts.

That distinction is a crucial one. Our class has had no lack of experience with what happens when someone who was once a union militant gets coopted into the alien class world of the officialdom and is no longer part of and help-

ing to lead a broadening movement of rank-and-file workers fighting the bosses. A compelling picture of how even
some of the best fighters can lose their souls was drawn by
Marvel Scholl—a decades-long SWP cadre, and a leader of
the women's auxiliary during the 1934 Teamsters battles
we talked about earlier—in a column she wrote for the
Militant a few years ago. It was headlined "The making of
a union bureaucrat."[25]

Becoming leaders of our unions

There are no hard-and-fast rules on tactical matters. But
we see no reason to change what we've said over the past
few years. Each specific case is a tactical question, but we
lean away from union officeholding today.

At the same time, we lean *toward* finding ways of being
responsible union militants, union builders, and union
leaders. Our aim is for our co-workers and ourselves to
use union strength—and, whenever possible, union structures—to fight for the interests of our class and its allies.
In the process, the ranks will be mobilized and the unions
will begin to change.

Sometimes this will take the form of helping to re-
vive moribund committees in the locals—civil rights
committees, environmental or educational committees,
participating in social committees, whatever. Sometimes
we'll help initiate new committees, as we've done around
the question of women's rights in some areas, or around
solidarity.

The bureaucrats want to nip everything in the bud, to
keep social thinking and politics outside the plants and
outside the union. *We want them inside.*

Our experience is that the industrial fractions that op-

---

25. Scholl's 1972 column is reprinted in this book on p. 147.

"At the Sparrows Point steel mill in Baltimore, party members, who function openly as socialists, are engaged in political activity with co-workers in two of the biggest USWA locals in the country."

Top: Newport News, Virginia, March 1979. Workers from Bethlehem Steel's Sparrows Point plant prepare to join rally in support of striking shipyard workers fighting for recognition of their union, USWA Local 8888. In photo, David Wilson, president of one of the two Sparrows Points locals, helps with sign.

Inset: Militant, March 16, 1979. Socialist newspaper, sold to working people across country, championed fight for union recognition.

Bottom: Baltimore, March 1978. Steelworkers and other unionists load food and clothing into trucks and cars as part of a 300-vehicle caravan to Martinsburg, West Virginia, in solidarity with nationwide coal miners' strike.

erate most politically and most audaciously are also becoming the best at trade union work, at participating with co-workers in job-related struggles, at drawing militants around them.

For example, the Milwaukee Road campaign is being organized through some extremely capable work within the official union structure—an ad hoc committee called together with official UTU sanction. As it turned out, however, the five workers who formed the initial core of the committee were all *Militant* subscribers. We're working with them on the Milwaukee Road drive, and they're reading our press—that's a good combination.

This is also happening at places like the Sparrows Point steel mill. Comrades operate openly as socialist workers and are at the same time helping to invigorate political activity in two of the biggest United Steelworkers locals in the country. They've helped initiate official union solidarity activities with the coal miners and Newport News strikes; helped establish active women's rights committees in both locals; held a union-backed forum on *Weber* at the union hall; got discussion going on plant safety; and helped transform some union meetings into political events that have an impact on the workers who attend them.

The same is true in USWA District 31 in Chicago, where we've been involved in Africa solidarity work, as well. It's true in Toledo, where comrades helped establish an official Solidarity Committee in their UAW local. It's true of many of our fractions.

And we've taken the first steps in building a United Mine Workers fraction, with party members working in coal mines in Pennsylvania, West Virginia, and Alabama.[26]

---

26. See "Trade Union Work and Party Building in the Coalfields," pp. 129–45.

We *do* compare these experiences with what the Minneapolis comrades set out to do in the 1930s. That is what we're trying to do, under today's conditions. That's who we're trying to emulate. Like the comrades and others who led Local 544, our eyes are on the ranks, not on "progressive" union officials.

We want to influence young workers. That's where we'll build our political current in the labor movement. That's where we'll find the initial cadres of the class-struggle left wing. That's where we'll win working-class fighters to the revolutionary program and the revolutionary party. And in the process, some union officials closer to the ranks may be won as well.

∾

Twenty-two. Comrades have made remarkable progress implementing the turn to industrial workers and the unions. Why? Because the party was politically prepared.

How we prepared for the turn

Looking back, the party leadership began preparations for this new stage of party building fifteen years ago. Farrell Dobbs was released from some of his responsibilities so he could follow the union movement more closely and write about it for the *Militant*. Farrell's articles laid the basis for our first major pamphlet on the unions in many years—*Recent Trends in the Labor Movement,* which we published in 1967. It's still in print.[27] Comrades should go back and read it.

Farrell wrote a number of documents for the Political Committee on key developments in the labor movement,

---

27. Reprinted as Farrell Dobbs, *Selected Articles on the Labor Movement* (Pathfinder, 1983).

as well. The whole party benefited from his memorandum adopted by the Political Committee in 1969 on Black caucuses in the unions, their meaning, the interpenetration of the Black radicalization with the labor movement. He drew up a resolution, adopted by our 1969 convention, applying our proletarian military policy to the fight against the Vietnam War and the growing opposition to the draft.[28]

In the process, Farrell also paid close political attention to aiding the transition in party leadership, which was necessary to successfully carrying out the turn.

We made a decision at the end of the sixties to ask Frank Lovell to leave Detroit and come back to New York to help organize our trade union leadership, and we gradually built up a national steering committee of knowledgeable comrades.

Party members working in rail joined in and helped lead the Right to Vote Committee in the United Transportation Union at the beginning of the 1970s. We responded quickly as a national party to the 1969 General Electric and 1970 federal postal workers strikes. We were prepared for Nixon's 1971 wage freeze and the 1973 meat and energy shortages. We correctly sized up the Coalition of Labor Union Women when it appeared in 1974, recognizing it as a sign of what was coming.

We began working more systematically with comrades in union situations. We developed sizable fractions of teachers and public workers, collaborating with them on a local and national level. These fractions aggressively took up the questions of racism, social service cutbacks, and

---

28. These documents by Dobbs can be found in *Selected Documents on SWP Trade Union Policy* and *Revolutionary Strategy in the Fight against the Vietnam War*, published by Pathfinder in 1972 and 1975, respectively.

independent labor political action that face teachers and public employee unions today. Comrades in the building trades, especially in the Bay Area, did important work, using their union base to build solidarity with labor battles and other progressive struggles. Our entire national cadre gained invaluable experience from these initial battles in the labor movement, and comrades won respect from their co-workers.

All these experiences and discussions found us ready to meet the opportunities of the Sadlowski campaign in 1976 and 1977, and for the National Committee decision in February 1978 on the party's turn to the industrial unions. Many comrades involved in these earlier experiences in the labor movement are now leading the building of our industrial union fractions.

So there was nothing sudden, nothing unthought-out, nothing unprepared. There were no surprises. Just a steady accumulation of experience and timely responses to changing situations in the class struggle itself.

Boston busing struggle

The party's national orientation toward the Boston desegregation struggle in 1974–75 was another crucial part of this preparation. We met with flying colors the test of a proletarian party—its ability to intervene effectively and decisively to advance the interests of the oppressed.

The Boston Black community fought the racists to a standoff and preserved the busing plan in that city, and we were part of that battle. Because of the relationship of class forces in Boston and in the Black movement, the struggle ran its course before a decisive victory could be scored. But a great deal was won nonetheless.

The Boston desegregation battle was the single most decisive political combat experience for an entire layer of

"To increase their profit rates, capitalists must intensify the exploitation of workers. They have no choice but to go after the industrial unions."

JACOB PERASSO/MILITANT

LISA AHLBERG/MILITANT

Top: St. Paul, Minnesota, June 12, 2000. Meatpackers march from UFCW union hall to Dakota Premium plant gate, in fight that won union recognition. Days earlier, workers organized sit-down strike to protest line speed-up that increased injuries.

Bottom: Los Angeles, March 1990. Striking Greyhound workers join Eastern Airlines strikers on picket line. Airline workers held out 686 days—"one day longer" than owner Frank Lorenzo, whose failed union-busting drive forced company into bankruptcy.

"There is a growing need for solidarity in face of the rulers' offensive. Strikes turn into political battles for the minds of the working class. Not only of the workers on strike but of the entire class."

TOM JAAX/MILITANT

LAURA FLICKER/MILITANT

Top: Austin, Minnesota, April 1986. Unionists from across the country join march of 5,000 to back what became a nearly one-year strike by UFCW Local P-9 against Hormel. Socialist workers nationwide built solidarity with strike.

Bottom: Mural on Austin Labor Center dedicated by Local P-9 to Nelson Mandela, imprisoned leader of South African freedom struggle. Giant display expressed identification of the fighting packinghouse workers with battle against apartheid regime.

Top: Miami, January 1990. Members of United Mine Workers on strike against Pittston Coal Group march with striking Eastern Airlines workers at Martin Luther King Day parade. In cities across the US, Machinists at Eastern and Pittston strikers joined together to strengthen each other's battles.

Bottom: In 2003 workers went on strike at Co-Op mine in central Utah. The coal miners, most of them Mexican-born, won broad labor support in their three-year battle to organize a union.

"We fight for solidarity with struggles of all the oppressed and exploited here and around the world."

PAT NIXON/MILITANT

PAT NIXON/MILITANT

Top: Los Angeles, April 1985. As part of nationwide actions, contingent of Machinists marches in demonstration supporting freedom struggle in South Africa. ***Left:*** In same action, members of Oil, Chemical and Atomic Workers protest US military intervention in Central America.

ARTHUR HUGHES/MILITANT

Above: Washington, DC, October 1986. March protesting US-organized war against Nicaraguan Revolution.

Solidarity with
Striking Teamster
Port Drivers

Full Protection
Status
NOW!

Top: York, Pennsylvania, March 1995. United Auto Workers pickets at Caterpillar plant explain their fight to Kenia Serrano, a leader of Cuba's Federation of University Students who was on US speaking tour. Strikers welcomed opportunity to learn about example of Cuban Revolution.

Bottom: Los Angeles, October 2018. Port drivers rally to win recognition of Teamsters as their union and to defend immigrant workers facing deportation if federal government ended their "temporary protection status."

"The civil rights and women's rights struggles not only heightened the self-confidence of oppressed layers of the working class. They advanced consciousness within the entire working class of common class interests."

NANCY COLE/MILITANT

Top: Wollongong, Australia, March 1984. Contingent in International Women's Day march demands Port Kembla steelworks end ban on hiring women. Campaign won wide support, forcing company to hire hundreds of women workers.

Bottom: Institute, West Virginia, June 1979. First national meeting of women coal miners, organized by the Coal Employment Project, drew 200 people including 75 miners who were women. From left: Paulette Shine, Betty Jean Hall, Connie Weiss, Mary Zins. The CEP, founded two years earlier, helped women get jobs in the mines.

NORTON SANDLER/MILITANT

BERNIE SENTER/MILITANT

Socialist miners in US and United Kingdom brought solidarity to fellow workers in each other's countries.

Top: North Yorkshire, England, June 1987. Women coal miners and other unionists from US visit British coalfields to learn about miners' resistance to government drive to close mines and break National Union of Mineworkers. They were hosted by Women Against Pit Closures, made up of miners' wives and other NUM supporters.

Bottom: Virginia coalfields, November 1989. Socialist coal miners from United Kingdom, Paul Galloway (second from left) and Jim Spaul (fourth from right), join pickets on strike against Pittston Coal.

"The weight and power of the unions must be brought into the fights for Black rights, women's rights, and affirmative action."

Denver, August 1993. Mobilization to defend abortion clinic from threat of attack by rightist opponents of women's rights.

Worker at Jaguar's auto assembly plant in Birmingham, England.

Pamphlet that socialist workers campaigned with in defense of affirmative action. *Weber* case was a legal challenge to provision in Steelworkers contract that set job-training quotas for Blacks and women. Many unions defended these measures, and in June 1979 Supreme Court upheld them.

the party leadership, including a big component of our leadership who are Black. Out of our work as part of that struggle and solidarity actions around the country, we won militant fighters for Black liberation, of all skin colors, to the socialist movement. Many of them are today helping to lead the party into industry.[29]

❦

Twenty-three. Our biggest political conquest of the 1960s and 1970s is that we built the kind of party that could size up changes in our class and make the turn to the industrial working class and unions when the time was right.

We recruited cadres capable of doing revolutionary political work in our class, cadres who could take the lead in fighting to transform the labor movement and build a revolutionary party of industrial workers.

We're not going through this experience in the SWP alone. This is an international experience, and that fact is registered here at our convention. By making this turn, we're setting an example for our entire world movement.

❦

Twenty-four. Every major question of *world* politics is also an *American* question. We inherit the legacy of the imperialist epoch. We are building a party in the strategic bastion, the stronghold of the world capitalist system. What we do—or don't do—will have a decisive effect on everything that happens in the world and *to* the world.

The ruling class is incapable of heading off the global crisis world capitalism has entered. The rulers can postpone showdowns. They can deal heavy blows to the workers. But they cannot prevent the battles or stop the crisis

---

29. See glossary: Boston desegregation struggle.

short of inflicting devastating defeats on the working class, in the course of which we'll have a chance to defend ourselves and advance a revolutionary course toward the conquest of state power.

What about the union bureaucracy? Can they keep the lid on American labor? While the union officialdom can lead us into defeat after defeat and maintain their grip, the bureaucracy is ultimately an extremely weak layer. That's the truth. But they also have the state power of the ruling class standing behind them. They don't just fall. When our class moves into high gear, we will divide the officialdom. Most of them will be swept aside, making way for militant leaders from the rank and file.

We don't promise a socialist revolution tomorrow or at any definite date. Our turn has nothing to do with prophecies or impatience.

But we *can* promise some things about what lies ahead. Lenin and Trotsky sketched a strikingly similar perspective in 1921 in their reports to the Third World Congress of the Communist International.

"The question, which is raised by many comrades abstractly, of just what will lead to revolution—impoverishment or prosperity—is completely false when so formulated," Trotsky explained. "Neither impoverishment nor prosperity as such can lead to revolution. But the alternation of prosperity and impoverishment"—the good times and the bad—"the crises, the uncertainty, the absence of stability—these are the motor factors of revolution."

Trotsky added that the "tranquil mode of existence" of the labor bureaucracy "has also exerted its influence upon the psychology of a broad layer of workers who are better off. But today this blessed state, this stability of living conditions," Trotsky said, "has receded into the past"—as is beginning to happen today.

"Prices are steeply rising, wages keep changing in or out of consonance with currency fluctuations. Currency leaps, prices leap, wages leap and then come the ups and downs of feverish fictitious conjunctures and of profound crises," Trotsky said.

"This lack of stability, the uncertainty of what tomorrow will bring in the personal life of every worker, is the most revolutionary factor of the epoch in which we live."

And Lenin, in his report, underlined *the political preparation* required of communist parties in face of such unstable conditions. "The more organized the proletariat is in a developed capitalist country," he said, "the greater thoroughness does history demand of us in preparing for revolution, and the more thoroughly must we win over the majority of the working class." That revolutionary course, Lenin added, is one "the broad masses . . . learn more readily from their own practical experience than from books."[30]

That's what we promise. Nothing less, nothing more.

The *victory* of the socialist revolution will depend on many factors, including what we and other workers do. But the battles are coming, the revolutionizing will occur, and they will decide a great deal about the future of the human race.

We're convinced that revolutionists of action are going to come out of the American working class by the thousands and hundreds of thousands. They're going to learn

---

30. Lenin's report, along with a report by Trotsky, to the 1921 Communist International congress are published in issue no. 12 of *New International* magazine. The quotes here by Trotsky are from his summary report to the 1921 congress, which can be found in *The First Five Years of the Communist International*, vol. 1, published by Pathfinder.

Marxism in giant leaps and bounds. And that brings us to our final point.

~

Twenty-five. Our task is to do just one thing—to build an American party that, together with our comrades around the world, can help lead these working-class fighters to wipe this bastion of imperialism off the face of the earth and open the road to the socialist future of humankind.

Trade union work
and party building in the coalfields

KEN SHILMAN

In a February 16, 1980, report to a meeting of Socialist Workers Party members working in coal mines in West Virginia, Pennsylvania, and Alabama, Ken Shilman reviewed the party's decision to get members into mining jobs in the late 1970s and to be part of the fight to strengthen the United Mine Workers union, organize workers, and build the party.

Shilman, a member of the party's National Committee, organized the work to build the coal fraction during its initial years. He was reporting on behalf of the Political Committee, which had discussed in detail the political course of the new fraction.

As a teenager Shilman had joined one of the first Freedom Rides to protest racially segregated bus terminals in the US South and participated in other actions of the civil rights movement. These experiences led him to join the SWP. Over the years he worked to involve GIs in the anti–Vietnam War movement; to mobilize solidarity with efforts to organize workers, from hospital employees in New York City to miners in the Appalachian coalfields and packinghouse workers in Austin, Minnesota; and to build and educate the communist movement in the midst of this activity.

Below is an excerpt from Shilman's February 1980 report. Pseudonyms used in the original report have been replaced here by the names of the party members involved in this party-building work.

Almost two years ago, in early 1978, our first three comrades were hired in the coal mines, all in separate mines. Until six months ago these three comrades—Mary Zins, Tom Moriarty, and Clare Fraenzl—constituted our national coal fraction. Today we have thirteen working miners, and we have recruited one laid-off miner.

Better still, we've made major steps toward building fractions; only a minority of comrades now working as miners are the only party member in the mine.

When the first comrades were hired, we had no experience in underground mining, and we didn't want to get ahead of ourselves. From day one we had the objective of getting known among co-workers for our political ideas, of being known as socialist miners. But we wanted our new fraction to be *effective* socialist workers, and we wanted to avoid needless victimization. Comrades had a lot to learn before starting to sell the *Militant* underground, talking socialism there, or getting involved in United Mine Workers politics.

Almost every day the fraction discussed this process of integration into the workforce, examining their concrete situations. They learned how to answer such questions as, "What's somebody from Boston doing in a coal mine in West Virginia?" They got known by other workers, made some friends, learned from the miners about coal and the UMWA.

That was a necessary first step. From there each comrade

had a different experience as they became known as socialists with political ideas on many questions.

Each of the mines was different. District 5 (western Pennsylvania) and District 31 (northern West Virginia) have different histories. District 20 (Alabama) is different from Districts 5 and 31. One mine can be very different from another in the same district.

Becoming an effective socialist worker

Mary Zins had been in the mine in Pennsylvania's District 5 for several months when the call went out for the July 9, 1978, Equal Rights Amendment march in Washington, DC. She was for it, and the fraction decided she should say so. Word spread, and she became "ERA Mary" in the mine.

Some miners liked it, and others harassed her because of it. As Mary made friends on that basis, it was only natural that she show some of these people the ERA coverage in the *Militant*. Through these discussions with co-workers, word spread that Mary was a socialist. Not because we wanted everybody to know as a matter of principle, but because that's the way word gets around in a lot of mines. Mary became known also as "Red Mary." She'd been in the mine about four or five months, and by then she'd gotten to know a lot of people.

The branch helped by organizing regular weekly sales outside her mine and talking to people about issues of the day, about socialism, and about the need to also organize ourselves politically—about a labor party. Branches did a lot to back up all our miner comrades in this way.

Some people in the mine were interested in her ideas. Others gave her a very bad time and hoped they could drive her out, in part because she was a woman. But as every comrade has had to do, she stood up for herself and won her right to be there and to have a different opinion.

Mary is known as a conscientious union militant, an effective opponent of the company, and a capable co-worker and organizer. This too was consciously thought out and worked on by the fraction. In her local Mary talked up the Jericol strike in Harlan County, Kentucky, pointing out its importance as far as organizing Eastern and Western coal and strengthening the union in face of the bosses' assaults.[1] She, along with other miners, got her local to pass a message of solidarity to the striking Steelworkers in Newport News, Virginia.[2]

At one point there was a dangerous situation in the cage [a mine-shaft machine, like an elevator car, used to transport miners and materials] at the mine where she worked. Water was dropping on live wires, and the company refused to do anything. There was a big discussion among the miners about what to do. Mary joined in the discussion and had some of the right answers. Word got around. After this, there was a push for Mary to run for the safety committee—not from us, but from other miners.

Another time there was a strike at Mary's mine over the company falsifying records on mine hazards. Mary was active in the strike, and the fraction decided this was the right issue and the right time for Mary to write an article for the *Militant* published under her name. She phoned her local leadership for quotes, to give them advance notice of the article, and showed it around when it was published.

Mary participated in discussions in the union on ques-

---

1. Members of UMWA Local 8771 at the Jericol Mine in Harlan County, Kentucky, waged a strike over mine safety, pensions, and higher wages from December 1977 through the latter half of 1979. Jericol's owners had refused to sign the national contract won by the UMWA during the 110-day strike in 1977–78.

2. See glossary: Steelworkers Local 8888 (Newport News, Virginia).

tions from democracy and safety to women's rights and nuclear power. She was elected an official representative to the UMWA Women's Conference in November 1979 and reported back to her local. I don't mean by all this that Mary said something on every single question that came up. Far from it, the fraction had to pick and choose what issues to speak on and which ones to campaign around.

It is Mary's conduct in her local and on the job that explains why she was elected a delegate to the UMWA convention in December 1979. There she spoke on one of the major debated questions—union democracy. Mary is probably one of the few women to ever speak at a UMWA convention. Afterward, she had to defend her votes and positions taken at the convention in reports to her local.

At the convention Mary sold seven copies of Pathfinder's antinuclear pamphlet by Fred Halstead and a couple of *Militants*. But she didn't go around the convention hall trying to hawk *Militant*s. That would have been foolish in light of the anticommunist atmosphere UMWA president Sam Church created.

Mary continues to have wide-ranging discussions with her co-workers, who are concerned about the military draft being restored, about the economy, Iran, their safety, their lives, and their futures.[3] She is known and respected by many people in her mine as a union activist, a person interested in the big social questions of the day, and a socialist—all rolled into one.

Winning respect as union militant

Tom Moriarty went through a similar process in his mine, which was in District 31 in northern West Virginia. When he started, he concentrated on learning the job and get-

---

3. See glossary: Iranian Revolution.

ting to know his co-workers, which of course takes time. He joined in discussions going on and eventually sold the *Militant* to some interested people.

The union local that Tom is in is not as open as Mary's. Meetings are smaller; there is much less discussion. The local isn't known for doing much. But Tom's mine has had a number of job actions. From participating in them, we learned a great deal that helped us understand the strengths and weaknesses of the UMWA.

About a year ago, the fraction decided that Tom's local was a good place to see if we could get the UMWA to organize a support meeting for the Jericol strikers I mentioned earlier. We thought maybe an example could be set for other locals in the district. We knew the UMWA international leadership did not want to make a crusade out of the Jericol or Stearns[4] strikes.

The lack of solidarity and support action for these two battles was part of the retreat of the leadership under previous union president Arnold Miller, who had first been elected in 1972 on the crest of the Miners for Democracy movement in the UMWA.[5] But we figured the struggle was

---

4. Workers at the Stearns mine in southeastern Kentucky voted by a 3-1 margin in 1976 to be represented by the UMWA. The unionization vote came just three weeks after a mine in Scotia, Kentucky—also owned by Blue Diamond Coal—exploded twice, killing twenty-six. The Stearns miners went on strike in early 1977 when Blue Diamond refused to recognize the UMWA contract provision giving union-elected safety committees the right to shut down production in face of unsafe conditions. After a three-year battle, the UMWA International Executive Board came to an agreement with Blue Diamond on another union representation election, in which members of the scab company union, who outnumbered the striking miners, were given eligibility to vote. The UMWA miners boycotted the rigged vote, held in May 1979. The strike ended soon afterwards.

5. See glossary: Miners for Democracy.

at a stage where it might be possible to get something off the ground—and it was worth trying.

It was important for the future of the UMWA to beat back the antiunion offensive in eastern Kentucky. We knew other miners would also understand that the drive would eventually be directed at stronger sections of the UMWA, as is happening now in southern West Virginia. Tom talked to his local president, and at the union meeting the president proposed reaching out to other locals in District 31 to organize a meeting to support the Jericol strike. For a while it looked like it could get going, but then the district leadership stepped in and put the kibosh on it.

After this Tom was the target of some red-baiting, as well as physical threats from right-wingers. But by this time he had won respect for many of the things he'd said and done day to day, and a layer of miners backed him up. Tom wasn't isolated, so the red-baiting fizzled.

A few miners wanted to continue the fight for the Jericol meeting. But the fraction decided to let it go rather than get in a fight that couldn't be won. We discussed this with others involved and convinced them. During the course of this struggle, Tom made several trips to Harlan County, met some of the miners there, and reported back to workers in his mine.

Another thing Tom was able to do was organize a get-together of miners interested in building the West Virginia meeting for South African trade unionist Drake Koka, who was touring the US in late 1978 talking about the place of workers and the unions in the fight against the white-supremacist regime there. Tom contacted a number of people in his mine and a few *Militant* subscribers in other mines and talked to them about apartheid in South Africa and its connection with US workers.

Tom got a number of them together at one of their

homes to discuss the question and how to build Koka's meeting in Morgantown. This helped not only in building that event, but even more in strengthening our contacts with a group miners who were Black. One of these miners later spoke at a Socialist Workers Campaign rally in support of Rosalinda Flint, the party's 1978 candidate for US Senate from West Virginia.

Another important experience Tom had was the support work he did for the Birmingham comrades who were attacked while selling the *Militant* at a mine portal.[6] Several miners who'd been looking to Tom and the *Militant* as a source of truthful information about their struggle and those of other workers were outraged when they heard that people were being physically denied their right to sell the *Militant*. As some of them put it, what they were particularly upset about was the idea of miners being denied the right to read the *Militant*. Tom organized a telegram campaign, and they all sent messages.

Tom also participated in discussions that came up at union meetings on safety, health, the convention, etc. As with Mary, the fraction discussed what to concentrate on, and Tom used his good sense on when to join in.

When we go into the mines, we have to prove to miners which side we're on. We have to show we're on the side of the union—the worker—and against the bosses. That's our side too, of course, but miners don't know that. How could they? They've heard the company's unanswered anticommunist lies for years, and they've watched various

---

6. In June 1979, while selling the *Militant* at the gates of US Steel's Concord coal mine in Birmingham, Alabama, Nelson Blackstock and Eric Flint were badly beaten by thugs armed with bats and wrenches. Members of the United Mine Workers around the country and other unionists condemned the company-inspired attack.

Maoist and other ultraleft currents who preceded us in the mines. When they hear you're a socialist, many initially assume you're against the union and will get in the way of fighting for miners' needs.

We show by our actions and our discussions that we are effective fighters for the union and for the working class.

Defusing a witch-hunt

Another example I want to give is that of our comrade in the mines in Alabama, Susan Ellis. Here we had some special circumstances. Susan started work in summer 1979, shortly after the anticommunist witch-hunt had reached its peak at the Jim Walter Brookwood No. 4 mine in Birmingham.

Our goal, of course, was for Susan to become known to co-workers as a socialist with ideas about all kinds of questions and proposals on how to fight for our class and win. But it was clear this would be a little longer process. We had to let the anticommunist atmosphere in Birmingham-area mines cool down some.

That assessment was confirmed when Susan started her two-week training course. A good part of the class time was taken up by the company instructor talking about the "commie girls" at Brookwood No. 4 and threatening to hurt or even kill any "commies" at his mine (I'll take up that incident later). The aim was to intimidate not just socialists but all women in the mine.

Our orientation was for Susan to make friends, learn about the union, become familiar with issues like safety and the Alabama surface mining laws. She did just that. She's gone through experiences from job grievances to a strike. She's known as a union person and as a miner who feels strongly, along with other women on the job, that women should have equal opportunity in the mines.

She was in a good position when the UMWA Women's Conference came in November 1979. She talked about it with some of her friends in the mine, and then with the local leadership. There was no objection, and she went to the conference. On coming back, she reported to a number of people who were interested, especially other women. She told people about the Labor for Equal Rights Now march in Richmond last month.[7] She worked to get people to go to the march, and went herself with the knowledge of some miners and the local leadership.

Susan isn't yet known in her mine as a socialist. But she's continuing to join in struggles that come along and doing political work around big social questions like the ERA. She'll continue to express her opinions on many questions. And when the time and the issue are right, she will tell some co-workers that all these views add up to being a member of the Socialist Workers Party.

∾

As more comrades have gotten into the mines in recent months, we relied on what we'd learned in our initial experiences. We went step by step with every comrade, integrating ourselves into the workforce, with full fraction discussions of each move. Far from blunting initiative, this gave comrades confidence to move as boldly as their situation permitted.

As part of the last two years' work, there's one national development in the UMWA that our small forces may actually have had an effect on—and that is the place of women in the UMWA. We are not an insignificant part

---

7. Labor for Equal Rights Now (LERN) was a coalition of trade unionists formed in Virginia in 1977 in support of the Equal Rights Amendment. On January 13, 1980, it organized a national demonstration of some 5,000 in Richmond, Virginia, for ratification of the ERA.

of this big change in the coalfields. In 1973 there were no women recorded as underground miners. Today there are over 2,500 underground miners who are women, and we have ten comrades who are women in the mines. If you think about that for a second, that's a pretty big percentage. We're an integral part of this new development.

As miners who are women began gaining a little confidence, and with the needed initiative and sponsorship of the Coal Employment Project (CEP), the first women miners conference was held in June 1979.[8] The day-to-day problems facing women in the mines were discussed, and comrades who were there say you could see women miners gaining more confidence as the conference went on. We—and "we" at that point were just two comrades, Mary Zins and Clare Fraenzl—played a key role in keeping the Maoists and others sects from engineering a setback to women's rights in the UMWA. The Maoists came with plans to use these women to attack the Miller leadership. We came hoping to facilitate this new development of union women fighting for their rights.

The subsequent official UMWA women's conference might not have happened at all if we hadn't proposed at the CEP-organized conference that the next one be sponsored by the union. This became very popular among women in the coalfields, and due to this pressure a national UMWA women's conference was called under Arnold Miller's sig-

---

8. The Coal Employment Project–sponsored gathering was held in Institute, West Virginia, near Charleston. Some 200 people participated, including 75 miners who were women from West Virginia, Pennsylvania, Illinois, Kentucky, Virginia, New Mexico, and Wyoming. The CEP had been formed in 1977 to help women get jobs in underground mines. Led by Betty Jean Hall, an attorney from eastern Kentucky, it also joined in solidarity with UMWA strikes and other union activity. As women's employment in the mines declined, the CEP ceased functioning in 1999.

nature for November 1979.

Despite the short notice, we built it in every way we could. Two comrades were sent to the conference as official delegates from their locals with assignments to report back to their local union meetings. Almost all the comrades brought co-workers to that conference.[9]

Our orientation was to advance the self-confidence of women in the mines and strengthen the class consciousness of miners concerning affirmative action programs—not to organize women miners as an opposition to the UMWA leadership. We introduced the Labor for Equal Rights Now march in January, in Richmond, to an enthusiastic audience. We sold *Militant*s and met a lot of people, some of whom we've stayed in contact with.

In almost every mine where we have comrades, we were able to take the LERN march to our locals. One local endorsed it. In some we raised it but didn't foolishly call for a vote, since it would have been defeated. But in almost all our locals there was a genuine discussion on just what is the ERA, what it means for men as well as women, what effect it would have on the seniority system, and so on.

Our most important work was done among our co-workers. The fraction went all out to build a UMWA contingent at the march, and it was very successful.

Lessons from a setback
We did have one major setback during our first two years of work—at the Jim Walter Brookwood mine no. 4 in Alabama. It was a setback of our own making. And it was a doozy. The miners fraction is responsible to itself and to

---

9. Seventy miners who were women participated in the UMWA-sponsored conference on "Union Women in the Mines," held November 10, 1979, in Charleston, West Virginia.

the party to make a clear assessment of what happened and why. And to draw the lessons.

When two comrades, Sara Jean Johnston and Ellen Bobroff, got hired at Brookwood no. 4 in June 1979, we walked into a war between Jim Walter mining company and the UMWA. Jim Walter was out to destroy the local. In a signed article printed in the *Militant*, Sara and Ellen described the situation by quoting Dave Lawson, the UMWA international safety inspector, who had given a report at the very first membership meeting of the union local that Sara and Ellen attended.

The authors quote Lawson as saying: "I never saw such a heap of [safety] violations in one mine in my life and the state won't do anything." The quote goes on: "Brothers and sisters, we've got a time bomb in this mine waiting to explode. And the only people who can stop it are you miners. We've got a safety clause in that contract book over there and we've got to force Jim Walter to honor that."

"Get it straight. When the UMWA filed charges against those foremen we declared war on Jim Walter and you better believe they're going to try to break you any way they can."

This was a fighting union local in battle for its life. In the two years we've been in the coalfields, we've experienced no other situation that came close to the stakes involved here. If Jim Walter could have broken this local, they had more mines in the Birmingham area that would have been next. That was the situation we walked into.

Another front in the fight, but secondary to the war over safety, was the company's efforts to weaken and divide the workforce by discriminating against women miners, many of whom were new to the mines. After a very short time on the job, our comrades became part of a grievance for back pay filed by the union on behalf of a number of women miners, and the grievance was won.

It is here, right at the beginning, that we started to make mistakes, which the entire fraction leadership takes responsibility for. Ellen and Sara are no longer working at the mine, but we invited them to this fraction meeting to join us in discussing this experience.

The central problem was that the fraction did not carefully and collectively think out and discuss the actions we were taking and the consequences for the union and the workers at Brookwood no. 4. We were new in that mine. We needed to size up the situation. We needed to listen and learn. We needed time to make friends and win respect as workers and union members.

By writing an article for the *Militant* about a closed union meeting, quoting extensively from a UMWA official, we set in motion an entire train of events. The fact that it was signed by two comrades who had only been working at the mine a few weeks greatly compounded the damage.

At the national fraction meeting in Ohio a week later, we deepened the errors. All the signals were there, and we should have seen them. But it wasn't clear to us that a war was going on at Brookwood no. 4 between the UMWA and the company. We needed to absorb that fact *before doing anything*. But we didn't organize any concrete discussion of what was happening at the mine. Instead, the fraction had a discussion about how, in general, comrades in the mines were finding ways to raise political issues and let people know they are socialists. The two comrades left the meeting with the idea they'd go back and show that issue of the *Militant* to some friends in the mine.

The national miners fraction had already had some experiences and discussions about signed articles on union meetings. With some consideration, we might have reversed the disastrous direction we were moving in. The fraction meeting should have drawn the lesson that it had been wrong to run the article in the paper in the first place, and then decided that comrades would *not* sell that issue in Birmingham and hope no one else sent it to the company.

The article gave the company and its right-wing agents the handle they were looking for. The red scare and violence that followed changed the relationship of forces dramatically. From a unified force fighting a war with the company, the union was turned inward; members began fighting each other over "communism." What the company had failed to do with its attacks on women's rights and other tactics, it pulled off with anticommunism. It divided the union and diverted the struggle from the war over safety.

That's not what we intended, of course, but it was the result. We got in the way of the miners' fight against the company and enabled the bosses to deal the union a major blow. We became an obstacle to strengthening the union.

Our actions also led to serious victimization of ourselves and other miners at Brookwood, who had their cars firebombed, tires slashed, and lives jeopardized. The climate of terror intimidated everyone. The co-workers who came to our defense were good people, courageous, and they helped us at great personal risk. But the fact that we weren't 100 percent isolated despite our newness and our mistakes doesn't justify what we did. The best layer of workers knew it would be an even bigger setback for the union if anybody was hurt by the right-wing thugs. They helped us for that reason.

We have to take responsibility for the damage done to other miners victimized due to our actions. The bosses don't play games. What *we do* has an effect on events and people, on their lives and livelihood. It is a sobering responsibility.

It was all these factors that led us to the party's decision that Sara and Ellen should get out of the mine.

As our party gets deeper into the working class and unions, and as more and bigger skirmishes in the class struggle occur, we will be confronted with these kinds of situations again. We will win political respect and recruit to our party on the basis of our program and our leadership capacities—demonstrated in our actions.

But leadership is not being in the limelight. It is the ability, alongside other workers, to lead our class to victories. We have to know the difference between a victory and a defeat. At Brookwood no. 4, there was no victory anywhere. The UMWA is not a weak union. But the struggle did suffer a significant setback.

The party also suffered a setback. We lost an opportunity to establish ourselves as serious and effective unionists and class-struggle fighters, to gain experience and to recruit to the party. We left a whole mine full of workers—and their co-workers and friends working elsewhere—confused about what the Socialist Workers Party is and open to the company's slanders against us, a situation we won't be able to change overnight.

What we must do now is to learn the lessons and move on with building our fraction. Our objective is to establish a big miners fraction in Alabama, and we are confident the Birmingham branch will be able to do so.

There are no guarantees against victimizations as we participate in the class struggle. That depends on the relationship of forces, which is beyond our control. Our job is to minimize *needless* victimizations of ourselves and, even more importantly, of those who come to our defense and remain behind when we're no longer there.

One important lesson is that tactics are always concrete. There are no universal formulas. Every step takes collective work and competent leadership. That's why we build fractions. That's why we have a party.

The making of a union bureaucrat

MARVEL SCHOLL

Scholl, a fifty-year cadre of the Socialist Workers Party, was a leader of the women's auxiliary during the 1934 strikes and organizing drive led by Teamster Local 574 (later 544) in Minneapolis, Minnesota. She served on the staff of the local's Federal Workers Section, which organized the unemployed to fight for their interests during the Great Depression. Scholl contributed to the *Northwest Organizer*, the Minneapolis Teamster weekly. In the 1960s and 1970s she wrote regularly for the *Militant*, including for many years the National Picket Line column. The following article appeared in the April 14, 1972, issue of the *Militant*.

The *Militant* has many new readers, many of whom have never belonged to trade unions. Therefore, it's possible that the words "bureaucrat" and "bureaucracy" applied to the organized labor movement may not have much meaning or may be confused with the government hacks who wrap everything up in yards of red tape in order to maintain the status quo.

While there are a great many similarities between the government and trade-union bureaucracies, there are almost as many differences, particularly in *how* each type of bureaucrat or bureaucracy got that way.

The trade-union officialdom, especially in the higher echelons, is composed of elected officers who have interpreted their own international constitutions in such a way as to practically perpetuate themselves in office—some of them for life, but most of them, in any case, long after they have outlived their usefulness. This is done by rigging the conventions where most international officers are elected or by questionable balloting procedures in referendum votes. But the men and women who make up this select coterie are not those I would like to discuss.

It is the men and women in the lower and middle echelons of the hierarchy, the business agents and organizers, that need examining. These people are charged directly with keeping the rank and file in order, riding herd on them in strike situations, and getting them out to vote for the Democratic "friends of labor."

Some of these lower-echelon union officials "got on the pie," as workers characterize getting on the union payroll, with malice aforethought—demonstrating their militancy in the plant primarily to further their own ambitions.

But many others got there by another route—being kicked upstairs in order to get them out of the hair of both management and the union hacks.

Let's take a not-so-mythical example of one militant trade-unionist who was turned into a typical bureaucrat.

Joe Jones worked on the line in an auto plant, alongside his best friend, Jack. Both men's families had a close social life. Jack was a good union militant, but not an aggressive one. He looked to Joe for leadership and supported him as the section grievance-committee man ("griever").

Joe worked hard attempting to settle the many beefs the rank-and-file workers had. He honestly believed in enforcing the contract to the letter.

Joe was a World War II veteran and joined the union after his discharge from the Army. He came from an old-line trade-union family. Both his father and his grandfather had been part of the great strike wave of the 1930s. He had listened to many stories from them about the days when the rank and file in these new industrial unions controlled their own leadership.

As a griever he tried to do his job. In the eyes of both the company and the local union hierarchy he became a "gadfly." At one point, angered at the growing number of unsettled grievances in his file, he fought with a foreman and was fired. Word went through the plant like wildfire and all the men walked off the job. Joe got his job back.

By now both management and the union hacks knew they had to do something about Joe.

Management decided to offer him a supervisory job— an old gimmick that sometimes succeeded in making the former union militant one of the best of company men.

But the union officialdom beat the company to the punch. They had discussed Joe and decided that the best way to handle him was to kick him upstairs, onto the union payroll.

After some hesitation, Joe accepted. He felt that in such a post he would be better able to help his own men.

He started out that way. His fellow organizers warned him that his efforts would be fruitless, but he tried anyway. He kept close contact with his former assembly-line friends, visited the job daily, tried to force definitive decisions on grievances and violations. In meetings with the management and union officials above him, he began to feel as though he were fighting two enemies.

He griped a lot and considered going back into the plant, but his much higher salary as a union hack got in the way. His family now had a new home in a much nicer neighborhood and a new car. This "better way of life" was changing Joe's whole outlook. He stopped visiting the plant every day, avoided the grievance-committee men who swarmed over him when he did come in, and spent less and less time socializing with his best friend, Jack.

He didn't like himself much, but held onto the idea that he could still do something concrete for the workers in the plant.

Gradually, he settled into his new role, began to accept the frustrations that went with it, and became just another lower-echelon bureaucrat—a "leader" with his eye out for promotions within the hierarchy.

His former close friends watched Joe change from a fighting militant into a well-trained, tamed, and contented union hack—one they could not remove. They hadn't elected him, so they had no recourse to the unions' constitutional provisions for recall.

More and more, Joe went along with the district and local union bureaucracy and the international leadership. He had been house-trained.

The turn and building a world communist movement

The report below was adopted in November 1979 by a world congress of the Fourth International.[1] Jack Barnes reported on behalf of the United Secretariat, the International's elected leadership body. The vote was 77 for, 17 against, with 19 delegates either abstaining or not voting.

Contrary to the course of the SWP and parties in several other countries, however, the leaderships of most of the organizations represented at the congress did not carry out the turn to industry that had been adopted, and political differences on other questions rapidly widened. By the late 1980s, the SWP and Communist Leagues in Australia, Britain, Canada, France, Iceland, New Zealand, and Sweden had each decided to end their affiliation to the Fourth International as it had evolved in order to continue to advance the proletarian internationalist course charted by Lenin and the founding leadership of the Communist International.

---

1. See glossary: Fourth International.

One central, practical consequence flowing from the political resolution submitted to this congress by the United Secretariat *overshadows all others*. The sections of the Fourth International must make *a radical turn* to immediately organize to get a large majority of our members and leaders into industry and into industrial unions.

I'm not going to review in detail the structural, demographic, and economic changes behind this decision. The political resolution points to the growing weight of the proletariat in all three sectors of the world revolution—the imperialist powers; the countries where capitalist social relations have been overturned; and the oppressed nations of Asia and the Pacific, Africa and the Middle East, and Latin America and the Caribbean. It points to the urban explosions and proletarian forms of organization that have been, and will continue to be, the focus of revolutionary upsurges in the years ahead.

Combined with these structural factors underlying the turn, there are two other considerations. On the one hand, there is the long-run stagnation the world capitalist system faces and the antilabor offensive it engenders. On the other, going into this crisis, the bourgeoisie faces an undefeated working class.

To this *capitalist* crisis must be added the growing crisis of *the world imperialist system*.

All this makes the world situation more, not less, explosive. It means that uncontrolled forces—spurred either by the actions of the oppressors or those of the oppressed—can be set into motion. We've seen this in Iran, Grenada, and Nicaragua over the past year. And this explosive potential is not limited to the semicolonial world.

Superimposed on these factors is another very important conjunctural factor, the world recession of 1974–75. This downturn was the first generalized recession on a world scale since the 1930s. What this definitively has set in motion throughout the world is an intensifying drive by the ruling class against the working class, against all the oppressed, and against the political rights the masses need to organize and fight back. This is not just a tactical or short-run policy of the rulers. It is a fundamental policy that economic realities *force* them to carry out.

The ultimate target of the rulers' austerity drive is the industrial workers, for the same reasons industrial workers have been at the center of our strategy since the founding of Marxism. These include the economic strength of the industrial working class; their social weight; the example they set for the whole class. Add to that the power of their unions to affect the wages, conditions, and thus the entire social framework of the class struggle; their resulting potential political power vis-à-vis the enemy class; the obstacle they pose to rightist solutions by the bourgeoisie.

The industrial workers are the source of most of the rulers' surplus value, which is divvied up among rival sectors of capital—industrial, banking, commercial, and others—through national and international competition. In today's crisis-ridden world of stagnating profits in the expansion of industrial plant and equipment, the weight of what Marx called fictitious capital is mounting in the division among competing capitalists of the wealth created by productive labor's transformation of nature.

Industrial workers are the producers of the biggest bulk of *all this surplus value*, whoever's hands it ends up in among rival capitalists—manufacturers, wholesale or retail traders, real estate interests, or bankers and financial speculators. The industrial working class is the ultimate enemy the capitalist rulers must defeat if the entire economic and social crisis of the their profit system is to be turned around.

The ruling class cannot afford for these industrial workers to organize *solidarity* with fellow workers, with the oppressed, and with their allies throughout the world. It cannot afford for the industrial workers to develop *trade union democracy,* so that the power of the working class can be organized and used—especially since the decisive use of that power can set an example for all the exploited and oppressed.

In other words, without a mighty battle, the rulers will not allow the evolution—*the organization*—of a *class-struggle left wing in the labor movement.*

The ruling-class offensive brings down increasing pressure on the entire working class, among national minorities, women, and every exploited and oppressed person fighting for their rights. It intensifies pressures on everyone seeking to chart a course forward, especially those seeking the revolutionary road, a class-struggle perspective, progressive alliances. Everyone seeking an independent working-class course feels this pressure. It is a fundamental aspect of the capitalist rulers' austerity drive, of their antilabor offensive, and one that will be magnified as the offensive deepens.

As the political resolution affirms, the only possible reversal of the capitalists' long-term crisis is through a large and decisive enough defeat of the industrial working class to rationalize and restructure capital, to attack with force every upsurge of the colonial peoples, and thus open a new period of expansion.

What conclusions must we draw from this in order to prepare? What probabilities must we act on?

That a political radicalization of the working class—uneven and at different tempos from country to country—is on the agenda.

That the rulers' offensive will force big changes in the industrial unions.

And that the key for revolutionists is to be in and part of the decisive sector of the working class, prior to these showdowns.

It is *there* that we will meet the forces to build the core of revolutionary workers parties. It is *there* that we will meet the young workers, the growing number of women workers, the workers of oppressed nationalities, and the immigrant workers. It is inside the industrial working class that revolutionary parties will get a response to our program and recruits to our movement.

It's also important to step back and look at the turn from a broader historical point of view. Our movement's current social composition is abnormal. This is a historical fact, not a criticism. In fact, far from being a criticism, it was our movement's ability beginning in the early sixties to recruit from the new generation of radicalizing youth, many of them students, that today poses the possibility of making this turn. And this *possibility* now coincides with a pressing political *necessity.*

Only parties that are proletarian not just in program, but also in composition and experience, can lead the workers and their allies in the struggles that are on the agenda.

Only parties of industrial workers will be able to withstand the pressures of the ruling class, including the ideological pressures. And these pressures will increase.

Only such parties will have their hand on the pulse of the working class, and thereby not misread their own attitudes, ignorance, and moods as those of the workers. In other words, only parties of industrial workers can move forward and outward.

Only parties of workers that have been tested *in action* by the workers themselves, well before the decisive showdowns, can grow and chart a way forward. Only that kind of party can attract and link up with the militant class-struggle currents that will break loose as the crisis of the reformist leaderships and centrist organizations deepens.

Marxism's proletarian continuity

We are not blazing a new trail in this regard. In the history of the Marxist movement, the most proletarian parties have been the best parties—the most revolutionary, the least economist, the most political. Go back to the Bolsheviks. Go back to Rosa Luxemburg. Go back to the goals the Fourth International set for itself, with the advice and leadership of Trotsky, at the end of the 1930s.

In fact, it is the proletarian tradition and orientation of the Fourth International that enabled us to arrive where we are today as a politically unified revolutionary organization on a world scale—an organization that has cadres to make this turn. And it's the turn—universally led and carried out—that is the only way to preserve and enrich our proletarian orientation.

At the same time, it is crucial to recognize and state clearly that the turn is *not* a continuation of what we've been doing worldwide. It is the way we can continue our proletarian orientation, but to carry out this turn on a world scale, we must make a break with what we've previously been doing. That's why we call it a *turn*.

This turn will dictate no tactics. Our tactics and campaigns in each country are dictated by the class struggle, by the conflict of class forces. But the turn affects every single one of our tactics, all our political work, all our institutions, and every single mode of party functioning. The turn is not a *sufficient* condition to take advantage of the opportunities before us and to meet the crises facing our class. But it is a *necessary precondition* for the next steps forward. Failing that, we can make no progress.

This is what the world political resolution lays out as the

central task for the entire Fourth International: to organize and *lead* the overwhelming majority of our cadres into industry and the industrial unions "without further delay."

"The goal," according to the resolution, "is parties of experienced worker-bolsheviks who act as political leaders of their class and its allies."

It goes without saying that we will not carry out the turn in exactly the same way in every country or part of the world, whether we have ten members or a thousand. But for the political and organizational reasons we've discussed, the turn is a *universal* one for our international movement, in all three sectors of the world revolution. That needs to be understood, so that we can carry out this task as a disciplined world party.

There comes a time when a political opportunity, a sociological fact, and a leadership decision coincide. This is one of those times. To put our movement in a position to move forward politically, we must simultaneously take our cadres and our program into the decisive sections of our class. Otherwise, we'll become *part* of the growing crisis of leadership in the world labor movement, rather than part of its solution.

Experiences and lessons

The political resolution for this world congress was drafted a little more than a year and a half ago. Since that time, our movement has had a great deal more experience with the turn. We've already had the chance to test our conclusions and develop a richer knowledge of the facts than we possibly could have had when we first adopted this resolution. This report and discussion will help us take cognizance of these experiences and changes and, if the report is adopted, present them in printed form to our entire movement.

Of course, there is unevenness from one country to the

next in the current stage of implementing the turn. There are differing stages in the development of the political situation in various countries. Some important experiences have been unique to a single section or a single industry. We can put those aside for today's presentation and discussion.

But there is an entire set of experiences that are common everywhere we have seriously begun the turn—from Iran to Canada, from Sweden to New Zealand. These common lessons are decisive everywhere we have significant forces in the Fourth International. They are lessons for the *practical leadership* of the next step forward in carrying out this common task.

What are these lessons of the last few years?

First. There is no possible way to make the turn unless the leaders of each party lead. This means that the leadership must analyze and effectively intervene in the unfolding of the class struggle, so that both the political basis of the turn and its practical application are always presented clearly to our cadres.

Comrades cannot be ordered or shamed to make the turn. They have to be politically convinced, inspired, and organized by the leadership. The membership is *waiting* to be led. That's our universal experience.

But this can only be accomplished if the leadership itself goes into industry. Our goal is not just to get a majority of the membership into industry, but a majority of members of our elected leadership bodies as well, on a local and national level. Only such a leadership can carry through the turn.

Second. The turn has to be approached collectively, not individually. Comrades aren't doing it on their own. They're not sent in to some workplace and then left to fend for themselves. Every time we've done that, we've reaped the whirlwind. We've lost comrades to demoralization, or to opponents, including the Stalinists. The turn is a conscious *party* task, not a routine task of a small group of comrades individually.

What is decisive in making the turn and practicing politics in industry is not what comrades accomplish as individuals, but what they accomplish as fractions and as part of the party. Comrades with different strengths and weaknesses work together as a disciplined unit of the party, learning from their joint successes and errors.

Third. Experience has taught us that there is no gradual way of accomplishing the turn. Of course, it takes place over a period of time. Comrades go into industry in successive waves, not all at once.

But the turn cannot be presented or implemented as a gradual, routine, or partial campaign. It must be organized and led as a decisive act by the entire organization. Whenever it has been tried any other way, the turn stalls to a halt and recoils, rather than going forward in waves. If we don't recognize this and act on that basis, we will fail.

When we gather the statistics from each national leadership for the next meeting of the International Executive Committee, we will get a feel for how much progress we're making—country by country—in leading a big majority of comrades into industry.

Fourth. In every single country where we've made progress with the turn, we've learned—sometimes from false starts—that there can be no such thing as current jobs or categories of jobs that are exempt, or layers in the party who are exempt. Such exceptions become excuses not to carry out the turn, not to participate in it. Trade unionists who are now working jobs *outside* industry—in the banks, schools, government employees, and so on—have a particularly important role to play in personally leading party cadres into industry and bringing their experiences to bear in building our fractions. They can provide essential political and practical leadership.

I think we've now bypassed a false debate—the debate over the public versus private sectors. What's important is not whether comrades are paid by the capitalists through their governments or by a private employer. What's important is that we are in factories, mines, mills, transport centers, communication centers—whether in the private or public sector. *Our goal is to get into industry, to become part of the industrial working class.*

We don't begin by looking for where most women currently are working or where the bureaucracy is weak. We look for where our class is concentrated and where class battles will, by necessity, open up in the coming period. That's where decisive class-struggle leadership will be needed and where we must go. That's the line of the resolution.

We are looking for leaders of the working class—those looked to for leadership by other workers. Some of them have already been elected to union posts, but our eyes are not on official leaders at any level. We'll win the best of them by going after the *young rebels* in the working class. They will be decisive for us and for our class in the coming period. That's who we want to recruit.

Fifth. This recognition of the centrality of young workers drives home the importance of launching, rebuilding, or helping to strengthen revolutionary youth organizations. Having a youth organization—and one fully geared into the industrial turn—becomes *more* important, not less important, as we concentrate our cadres in industry and the industrial unions.

The world Marxist movement has traditionally recognized the need for proletarian youth organizations as a central party-building instrument. As young industrial workers are repelled by capitalism and attracted to radical ideas and alternatives, this need becomes more pressing. We're learning that we must consciously recognize this as part of the turn in order to tap the opportunities before us and make the maximum gains for our parties among radicalizing workers.

What not to expect
Our initial experiences with the turn have also taught us what we should tell comrades *not* to expect.

We can't promise rapid recruitment. That depends on the unfolding of the class struggle, the stage of class politicization, and the capacities of the party.

We make no promises that the turn will solve other problems facing the party. We can guarantee, however, that the turn puts us in the best position to solve those problems and take advantage of opportunities. Without the turn, we can guarantee disaster.

And finally, we don't promise that the turn will be painless or easy. It won't be. It's unlike anything we normally do and have become accustomed to. It's not a change in political line or a correction of a political error. It's not a shift in tactics. It's not the launching of a new campaign.

The turn means changes in the lives of thousands of comrades. That's different. And it takes leadership.

Everywhere we've begun to carry out the turn in a systematic and thorough way, we have lost some individual comrades. There are those for whom the turn sharply poses the question of what they are doing with their lives, what their personal commitments and priorities are.

But the more important lesson we've learned is that the turn *saves* comrades. It prevents demoralization and turns around the malaise that sets in when our parties don't have the necessary political and organizational moorings in the heart of our class. It provides a perspective, and a realistic base from which to move our work forward. Unsuspected capacities in comrades come to the fore as they get into industry as part of a strong fraction.

That's a crucial aspect of the turn, and another reason why it must be carried out quickly and led decisively.

Some organizational conclusions

From our initial experiences, we have also drawn some conclusions on important organizational questions connected with the turn. All the organizational forms of our parties have to be subordinated to carrying out the turn.

One. Comrades who go into industry have to function as fractions, as a unit, together—whatever the particular term may be in different organizations in our world movement. Comrades have to have formal, structured ways to make decisions democratically, to be tied together politically, to work out problems, and to integrate and develop new comrades who go into industry or are recruited there.

If this does not happen, we can isolate, demoralize, and finally lose comrades. They begin to feel personally responsible for making party gains and personally to blame for any failures or setbacks. This is how we carry out work in every other arena, and that's how we must carry out the turn. It is crucial to organize and lead comrades through fractions. And the party leadership must pay close attention to their work.

Two. As we get more and more comrades into industry, it is crucial for the party leadership to maintain our basic units—our branches, or whatever we may call them—as *rounded political bodies*. They must be of sufficient size, and they must be organized politically, so comrades obtain something there they cannot get through the industrial fractions. These basic party units must provide the rounded political experience, leadership, Marxist education, and political discussion that comrades can only get from the party as a whole.

Failure to do this can even become an obstacle to combining what is often called trade union or factory work with more general socialist political activity.

Of course, this doesn't solve any of our tactical problems of how to link factory work, trade union work, with other party tasks and campaigns. Those will be solved concretely in each organization and specific situation.

But organizing comrades in industry to function as active members of rounded political units of the party—in which they have regular and systematic political decision-making power and responsibilities—is key to avoiding unnecessary pitfalls.

Three. The turn both necessitates further professionalization of the party and helps accomplish that goal. The turn makes more immediate and real our norm that every comrade, every worker-bolshevik, is a professional revolutionist. As we become parties of industrial workers, it's more necessary than ever to have an apparatus, that comrades be willing to take full-time assignments, and that we advance proletarian professionalism—not sloppy bohemianism—at every level of the organization.

At the same time, it is important to avoid any tendency to begin acting as if there are two categories of party members—those in industry and those not in industry. All party members have equal rights and equal responsibilities. The turn in no way establishes second-class membership for comrades who for whatever reason are not currently working an industrial job. We will pull comrades out of industry to take full-time assignments, and vice versa.

Four. The turn also brings into sharper focus the question of leadership norms and party norms in general. They must be reviewed to make sure they are in step with our advance along the historic line of march of our class.

Trotsky wrote a series of letters about these matters to the American comrades in the years leading up to the fight with the petty-bourgeois opposition in the late 1930s, when the party was carrying out an industrial turn. Most of these letters dealt with the leadership question.[2]

These were not moral lectures. Trotsky considered changes along these lines to be a precondition to building proletarian parties and a revolutionary international. In one 1937 letter he wrote: "I have remarked hundreds of times that the worker who remains unnoticed in the 'normal' conditions of party life reveals remarkable qualities in a change of the situation when general formulas and fluent pens are not sufficient, where acquaintance with the life of workers and practical capacities are necessary."

In a letter a few days later, Trotsky spoke of the need to educate the party in a spirit that "rejects unhealthy criticism, opposition only for the sake of opposition." The key to this is "to change the social composition of the organization—make it a workers organization."

Workers, Trotsky said, are "more patient, more realistic. When you have a meeting of 100 people and between them 60–70–80 are workers, then the 20 intellectuals, petty bourgeois, become ten times more cautious on the question of criticism. It's a more serious, more firm audience."

The petty-bourgeois intellectuals' tendency to criticize for the sake of criticism, says Trotsky, is a way to "muffle

---

2. The quotations from Trotsky that follow can be found in his October 3, 6, and 10, and December 8, 1937, letters, reprinted in James P. Cannon et al., *Background to 'The Struggle for a Proletarian Party'* (Pathfinder, 1979), pp. 13, 17, 18, 20.

their inner skepticism."

"The young workers," he says, "will call the gentlemen-skeptics, grievance-mongers, and pessimists to order."

Full-timers in a revolutionary organization, Trotsky stressed, "should have in the first place a good ear, and only in the second place a good tongue." And as the party begins to recruit industrial workers, Trotsky warned, it must "avoid a great danger: namely, that the intellectuals and white-collar workers might suppress the worker minority, condemn it to silence, transform the party into a very intelligent discussion club but absolutely not habitable for workers."

Awareness of these questions of attitudes and conduct is a necessity if we are to carry out the turn to the end. But it's more than that. By leading through the turn, we will have the greatest chance to alter the orientation, combat alien class attitudes, and improve the atmosphere and functioning of our parties. We will begin acting as parties of industrial workers.

Educate, agitate, organize

Five. The education of the party. As comrades begin the turn, they learn and relearn our program, learn and relearn Marxism. They are constantly challenged to explain and popularize our ideas to their co-workers. So we are obligated to expand and pay more careful attention to political education.

This is a safeguard against any susceptibility among comrades to move away from being political as the turn is being carried out. History tells us this is a danger.

Six. Improving our newspapers and turning them more and more into workers papers. It is through our party press that we can speak to the largest number and broadest layers of workers. It's how we explain that the labor movement needs to begin thinking socially and acting politically—that it's a life-or-death question.

Our own members are the single most important audience for the party press, along with those in our class and among the oppressed who look to us for political analysis and leadership. What we put in our newspapers, and how we explain our program, helps us train our cadres as worker-bolsheviks rather than radical trade unionists. It helps steel the party against economist tendencies to reduce the struggles of the allies of our class—women, the oppressed nationalities, farmers and other exploited producers—to union struggles or to struggles between employees and employers.[3] It helps combat any false ideas that international questions or broad political issues aren't of interest to workers and can't be presented to them effectively.

Seven. The turn makes more important, not less important, the building of *campaign parties*—parties that carry out centralized political campaigns dictated by the national and international class struggle.

We need parties that speak politically to the working class through our actions and our political campaigns, not primarily through how we relate to issues or struggles on the job. As the turn is made, these party campaigns are vital safeguards against rightist and economist pressures that have historically affected revolutionists in the working class.

If there is one thing that the turn does not change, it is our absolute opposition to any spontaneist concepts that a revolutionary leadership will somehow blossom of its own accord when the time for decisive action arrives.[4] To the

---

3. See glossary: Economism.

4. See glossary: Spontaneism.

contrary, a steeled and tested party needs to be built right *now*. That's the only way to be ready when those times do arrive.

Eight. We have begun to learn valuable lessons about the relationship of the turn to our participation in building actions that advance the struggles of women and oppressed nationalities, as well as international solidarity. We've learned not to confuse our trade union or factory fractions with our fractions set up to lead work in various other social and political struggles.

Of course, there is an interlinking. There is a crossover of membership. But we can't reduce one organizational form to the other to carry out our work. To do so simply reflects internally the tendency to reduce struggles by allies of the working class and other oppressed and exploited layers to battles in the factories or the unions. Our turn is a turn outward, not inward.

Struggles that develop inside and outside the labor movement need to be combined and mutually strengthened. Our turn, and the political factors underlying it, expand the possibilities for industrial workers and their unions to be brought into these struggles, not only as participants and leaders but more and more as conscious revolutionary leaders of the labor movement as well.

We can say in all truthfulness to the oppressed, "Your struggles must not be subordinated to any other struggle." It's only a revolutionary leadership of the working class that can say this and *act* on that basis. This is crucial to the ability of the working class to forge lasting alliances in a common battle against the exploiters.

Nine. We have discovered that where the turn has been carried through, women comrades and comrades of the oppressed nationalities develop more confidence in the party, as they gain more confidence in themselves. More confidence, not only as leaders of their particular struggles but as leaders of the working class and, above all, as leaders of the party.

The turn brings out the best in comrades.

Our turn toward the industrial working class and unions can also help solve the crisis of leadership in the movements of women and the oppressed nationalities. Today these struggles confront a crisis of class perspectives, as their current leaders cave to the petty-bourgeois pressures of their milieus and, even more than usual, look to courts and bourgeois politicians to advance their interests. They need to develop a proletarian composition, orientation, and leadership to move their struggles forward. As partisans and participants in these struggles, we will help accelerate the resolution of the leadership crisis from our base in industry, involving other workers in these movements and fighting to bring the power of the labor movement behind them.

Answers to some questions

I want to end on some questions that have been raised about the turn.

Is it mechanical? Is it a gimmick? Is it a factory obsession?

Well, I guess you could say we have a certain obsession about getting large fractions of comrades into great concentrations of industrial workers. We might quibble over the word. But we plead guilty.

Is it mechanical? Yes, in a certain sense. The mechanics of actually carrying through the turn are a precondition for its political success.

Is it a gimmick? No. It's not a gimmick. Unless our entire political analysis is wrong.

The leadership of the Fourth International, the International Executive Committee, must lead the turn.

It must lead through political analysis, in order to situate the turn in the unfolding world class struggle.

It must lead by more of its members going into industry.

It must lead through coordination of the turn on a world scale, facilitating the exchange of experiences and information among the national leaderships and comrades in industry in different countries.

This means that the IEC, like all other leadership bodies of our movement, will have to begin organizing its work differently. The agendas of its meetings will change. The questions it considers and deliberates on will broaden.

For example, the next IEC meeting must concretely look at the statistics on the progress of the turn and assess their political and organizational implications.

The only way the success of the turn can be measured is to look honestly and cold-bloodedly at the figures—the number and percentage of comrades in industry in each section, the number of functioning industrial fractions, the number of leadership cadres who are carrying out the turn. Only by reviewing these facts can we judge our progress in carrying out the central decision of this congress. This is what we must do at the next IEC meeting.

The more successful we have been in drawing the lessons and implementing the resolution, the quicker the turn *per se* will be behind us. The turn is a radical *tactical* move necessitated by the historical development of our movement and the current stage of world politics. It is an abnormal response to an abnormal situation—a situation in which the big majority of our members in every section have *not* been industrial workers. Once this historically necessary tactic has been carried out—once the abnormal situation of our current social composition and arena of work has been changed—the turn will be behind us. If it is carried out, the tactic has done its job.

Several comrades have told me, "Don't forget to point out that our movement faces a crisis, that we have a great number of problems." There's an important factor to remember in connection with this. The problems we face don't reflect decisive setbacks for the working class such as those in the 1930s—the rise of fascism and march toward world war—or a political retreat such as that in the 1950s.

The crises and problems we face today are ultimately rooted in our need to prepare for challenges and opportunities posed by an ascending class struggle and a situation in which the balance of forces on a world scale is shifting to our class. These struggles have not been decided. The biggest ones are still to come. And they are going to bring forward new forces from our class and its allies.

Building a mass world party

Given these revolutionary prospects, the turn is also decisive in putting the Fourth International in the position to accomplish what will be the most important challenge in building a mass world party of socialist revolution.

Everywhere we exist in the world today, we have only small propaganda groups. To accomplish the tasks we've set for ourselves, we must be able to turn to layers of revolutionists that come from other directions and other traditions—*revolutionists of action* such as those that came out of the Cuban Revolution and opened a renewal of proletarian leadership in power for the first time since the late 1920s. A renewal of communist leadership.

Or leaders of the revolutionary governments in Nicaragua and Grenada today. Or of left currents that arise from the crisis in the union movement and in the reformist Stalinist and Social Democratic parties.

Our capacity to work with these revolutionary-minded

workers, to attract them to our program and convince them of its necessity, to merge our forces and theirs into a common political framework—this is the only way we will build mass proletarian parties and a new communist International. It can't be done simply through individual recruitment.

But this historic task can be accomplished only by organizations firmly rooted in the working class with the large majority industrial workers. No party lacking that class composition will be able politically to stay the course.

We often point out that even relatively small revolutionary parties can grow tumultuously during mass upheavals, being forged out of the fighters that come forward in these class battles. This is true. That's what happened to the Bolsheviks in 1917.

But this can *only* be true for proletarian parties whose cadres have already been tested in action and have experience and respect in the workers movement. It cannot happen outside the heart of the industrial working class. Those who are on the outside when such developments occur will simply be bypassed. The opportunity will be lost.

This is the goal of the turn. To place our cadres where they must be to build workers parties that are capable of growing out of the big class battles that are on the agenda throughout the world. Otherwise, our program, which the world proletariat needs to chart a course to victory, will remain a lifeless document rather than a guide to mass revolutionary action.

We make no guarantees that the turn will bring us correct tactics, timing, or political savvy in meeting such opportunities. That will be up to the comrades on the spot in each organization and each new situation. We simply guarantee that these decisions *cannot* be made correctly without the turn, without parties composed in their overwhelming majority of industrial workers.

Finally, we should dispense with one myth. I was struck by it when reading an exchange between leaders of an ultraleft sectarian group, the British Socialist Workers Party, and comrades from the Fourth International group in Britain, the International Marxist Group. The British SWP warns that several years ago their American organization, the International Socialists, tried to place the big majority of its comrades into industry and the experience ended in disaster. Here's what they had to say:

> Now, while we completely agree with the *objective,* the solid implantation of revolutionaries in the industrial working class, we believe that the *method* proposed to achieve it can only lead to disaster. "Proletarianisation" or "industrialisation"—i.e., transplanting ex-students into industry—is only a substitute, and a dangerous one at that, for the real task of building workers parties.
>
> "Industrialisation" has certain superficial attractions. It yields quick results—it leads to significant increases in the number of manual workers among the members. These results are however achieved at a high price. The petty-bourgeois comrades sent into industry are forced to adapt to their new environment. Their first priority is to make themselves acceptable to their work-mates. The natural consequence is that they play down, or completely conceal their politics and concentrate upon making themselves effective trade unionists.
>
> A gulf opens up between their life as revolutionaries and their life as worker militants. Within the workplace their priority is not to win over other workers to revolutionary politics, to sell the party's paper, to present a programme of struggle against the bosses, but to establish themselves as good militants pure and simple. Within

the organisation they often become a conservative force, tending, for example, to take what they believe to be a "super-proletarian" (i.e., reactionary) line on questions of, for instance, sexual oppression, and to adopt generally economistic positions.

At the same time, "industrialisation" tends to create two tiers of membership within the organisation. There are the "worker-Bolshevik cadres" who have made the transition from petty bourgeois to "proletarian" and who therefore tend to regard themselves as an elite, and the rest, who exist, not to build the party and rank-and-file organisations in their own workplaces, but to "service" the "proletarians." Work in the white-collar unions and among students, far from negligible spheres of activity, tends to suffer severely under this sort of regime.

We are not inventing this scenario. It has happened in odd instances within our own organisation. It happened to the International Socialists in the United States, where "industrialisation" created a paper which hardly mentioned politics, a bloated full-time apparatus, a conservative layer of "proletarianised" students and, at the bottom, demoralised white-collar workers and students. The end result is that the organisation has dissolved itself into various rank-and-file union caucuses and a monthly propaganda magazine.

The conclusion the British SWP draws from this experience is: *Don't go into industry. The turn is wrong.*

We say just the opposite. We say the reason the International Socialists experience led to failure—and it was abysmal—was because of the program and leadership of the organization that carried it out. That leadership counterposed going into industry and "union work" to the development of a politically rounded workers paper,

Marxist education, and systematic political campaigns. When they made the turn, the leadership consciously *depoliticized* all party institutions. That's why they failed.

If such false counterpositions are made, then the turn will fail. You will lose comrades. And you won't recruit and hold young workers who are becoming political. If the party is falsely told to *choose* between an effort to get comrades into industry and carrying out organized political campaigns, then, of course, colonization will fail.

We have a different approach. We don't think comrades who have been recruited from and trained in important protest movements and struggles of the oppressed will become less political when they become industrial workers and union militants. We don't think they will stop fighting for women's emancipation and other social and political goals in the interests of the working class. Our experience already confirms that comrades become more confident and more effective in these struggles.

Ultimately, underlying opposition to the turn—whether consciously or not—is the prejudice that somehow workers are inherently less revolutionary, less political, and more intolerant than other sectors of the population. That's unqualifiedly false.

We are convinced that workers are *not* less political than other sectors of the population. To the contrary, as the struggles of all the oppressed deepen, industrial workers will more and more take the lead.

But to carry out the turn, we have to face facts. We have to look cold-bloodedly, honestly, and thoroughly at our current size, composition, and problems. There are no tricks or formally correct definitions that can help us become parties that are proletarian in composition as well as program. We have to start from our *real* composition, so we can judge the real tasks and opportunities before us.

Meeting the opportunities
There is no reason for pessimism. We should look at the crisis we face and the problems we confront as reflections of a period that is opening in which we can *resolve* them. The turn will give us the political perspectives we need to grow and move forward.

On a world scale, we are the only organized revolutionary alternative for the labor movement. Every other international current has failed.

We are convinced that in making the turn to the industrial working class, we must simultaneously build our national parties *and* an international organization. We cannot build revolutionary workers parties anywhere in the world without that internationalist course.

And a world communist movement cannot and will not be built unless its components are *workers parties,* rooted in industry, in countries throughout the world.

In politically leading the turn, we open the door to the entire next stage in constructing the international party of socialist revolution that is needed by the working class to topple world capitalism.

'Communism is not
a doctrine but a movement'

The following is from the report by Jack Barnes on the resolution "Building a revolutionary party of socialist workers" adopted April 29, 1979, by the SWP National Committee.

What is Marxism? What are we all about?

In October 1847, as part of his preparation together with Karl Marx to draft the Communist Manifesto two months later, Engels wrote a couple of editorials responding to a petty-bourgeois German socialist named Karl Heinzen (whose place in history lies in the fact that he served as a foil for Marx and Engels).

"Herr Heinzen imagines communism is a certain *doctrine* which proceeds from a definite theoretical principle as its *core* and draws further conclusions from that," Engels wrote.

"Herr Heinzen is very much mistaken. Communism is not a doctrine but a *movement*; it proceeds not from principles but from *facts*."[1] That's where the proletarian party's program comes from, Engels said.

Marx and Engels incorporated this central concept at the heart of the Communist Manifesto, which they had been asked to draft at the founding congress of the world's first modern revolutionary workers organization, the Communist League, held in London in December 1847.

"The theoretical conclusions of the communists are in no way based on ideas or principles that have been invented, or discovered, by this or that would-be universal reformer," they wrote. "They merely express, in general terms, actual relations springing from an existing class struggle, from a historical movement going on under our very eyes. . . ."[2]

Marxism is "simply" the generalized interests, written down, of one of the two major classes involved in that struggle in the modern world—the working class.

Communists "have no interests separate and apart from those of the proletariat as a whole," Marx and Engels wrote in the Communist Manifesto. "They do not set up any sectarian principles of their own, by which to shape and mold the proletarian movement."

Marx and Engels went on to pinpoint the internationalism of the communist movement, and its task in overcoming the national and other divisions imposed by capitalism on the working class.

"The communists are distinguished from the other working-class parties by this only," they say: "(1) In the national struggles of the proletarians of the different countries, they point out and bring to the front the common

---

1. Frederick Engels, "The Communists and Karl Heinzen," in *Collected Works*, vol. 6, p. 303.

2. Karl Marx, Frederick Engels, *The Communist Manifesto* (Pathfinder, 2008), p. 47 [2018 printing].

interests of the entire proletariat, independently of all nationality. (2) In the various stages of development which the struggle of the working class against the bourgeoisie has to pass through, they always and everywhere represent the interests of the movement as a whole."

Marx and Engels conclude: "The communists, therefore, are on the one hand, practically, the most advanced and resolute section of the working-class parties of every country, that section which pushes forward all others; on the other hand, theoretically, they have over the great mass of the proletariat the advantage of clearly understanding the line of march, the conditions, and the ultimate general results of the proletarian movement."[3]

Marxists *are part of* the working class, not something outside of it. The revolutionary Marxist party analyzes *all* classes and their conflicts, all politics, from the point of view of the historic goals of *our* class—the class we are simply the most conscious and organized part of and the most consistent fighter for. The class whose task is to govern, expropriate the exploiters and oppressors, and lead a great social movement to reorganize society to eliminate oppression and lay the foundations of a socialist society—changing ourselves utterly in the process.

The revolutionary working-class leader Malcolm X explained this transformation through struggle with exemplary clarity only a few weeks before his assassination in February 1965. A reporter asked him: Was his goal to "wake [African Americans] up to their exploitation?" Malcolm replied, "No, to their humanity, to their own worth."[4]

---

3. *Communist Manifesto*, p. 47.

4. Interview in the February 25, 1965, issue of the *Village Voice*, a New York weekly. Reprinted in *Malcolm X: February 1965, The Final Speeches* (Pathfinder, 1992), p. 295 [2018 printing].

The working class is created by its enemy—the capitalist class, the profit system. Workers don't *choose* to participate in the class struggle, we are *forced to* by our condition. By the fact that our tools, our use of the land, not only "forty acres" but the "mules" are taken from us.

This is what makes Marxism scientific, not utopian. And more and more workers in this country are becoming conscious of this class struggle as the rulers' offensive escalates—every day in the factories, and around the big social and political issues such as unemployment, discrimination, and war.

No wonder Marx and Engels wrote—in one of their earliest works, more than two years before workers recruited them to the world's first modern communist party—that there comes a stage in capitalist social relations "when productive forces . . . are brought into being" that "are no longer productive but destructive forces."[5]

This communist perspective and strategy for working-class independence and political power—that's all Marxism is. Of course, that "all" encompasses the future of humanity: the transformation of the great mass of humanity and the salvation of our planet from capitalism's "forces of destruction" and from the devastation of our conditions of life and work.

---

5. Marx and Engels, "The German Ideology," in *Collected Works*, vol. 5, p. 52.

GLOSSARY
OF NAMES, ORGANIZATIONS, AND EVENTS

AFSCME – Known since 1936 as American Federation of State, County and Municipal Employees; founded four years earlier as Wisconsin State Administrative Employees Association.

AFT (American Federation of Teachers) – Along with National Education Association (NEA), one of two major US teachers unions.

Angola – In late 1975 Angola's government, newly independent from Portugal, appealed for international help to resist invading army of US-backed white-supremacist regime in South Africa. Cuban government responded. Some 425,000 Cubans volunteered for duty in Angola over next 16 years. In 1988 South African army was dealt crushing blow by Cuban, Angolan, and Namibian combatants at battle known as Cuito Cuanavale, securing Angola's sovereignty, winning Namibia's independence, and giving powerful boost to overturn of apartheid in South Africa in the early 1990s.

Bishop, Maurice – *See* Grenada Revolution.

Black lung disease – Incurable, often fatal disease caused by inhaling dust from coal and silica. In 1960s and early '70s, initially spurred by fight to reverse black lung, rank-and-file coal miners organized powerful insurgency in United Mine Workers to replace UMWA bureaucracy that was in league with coal bosses. Through walkouts and mass protests organized by Black Lung Association, Disabled Miners and Widows, and Miners for Democracy, they won state and federal limits on dust levels, company-funded clinics, and above all union safety committees empowered to shut down production in face of health and safety violations. Black lung cases fell more than 90 percent from 1970s to mid-1990s. As companies shut down union mines with no offsetting UMWA organizing efforts, and safety committees were weakened or ended, black lung sharply revived; 20 percent of miners in Appalachia had disease in 2017, with substantial rise among workers with fewer than 10 years in mines. *See also:* Coal strike (1977–78); Miners for Democracy; UMWA.

Bolsheviks – Revolutionary proletarian faction in Russian Social Democratic Labor Party, formed 1903 under V.I. Lenin's leadership. In October 1917 led workers and peasants to state power in former tsarist empire. Renamed Russian Communist Party (Bolshevik) in 1918. Its leaders launched Communist International in 1919. *See also:* Communist International, Worker-bolsheviks.

Boston desegregation struggle – Federal court in 1974 ordered desegregation of Boston public schools, including busing Black children to better-funded schools from which most had been kept out. As classes began, top Democrats in Boston City Council organized thugs to launch violent attacks on school buses and against Blacks on streets and beaches. Over next year and a half, these assaults were beaten back by mass meetings, street demonstrations, and organization of bus marshals— backed by NAACP, National Student Coalition against Racism, sections of union movement, Socialist Workers Party, Communist Party, and others.

Brown, Bill (1897–1938) – President of Minneapolis Teamster Local 574 from 1921 to his death. Part of class-struggle-minded leadership of 1934 strikes that won union recognition for truckers and warehouse workers there and used it to expand union power in Upper Midwest and beyond. Supporter of Communist League of America, forerunner of Socialist Workers Party, but never a member. *See also:* Teamsters (International Brotherhood of Teamsters); Teamster series.

Burkina Faso – West African country where August 1983 popular uprising brought to power revolutionary government led by Thomas Sankara. Working people and youth mobilized to carry out literacy and vaccination drives; sink wells, plant trees, erect housing; combat women's oppression; begin transforming exploitative land relations. They began to throw off imperialist yoke and backed toilers' fights from Angola and South Africa to Nicaragua, Grenada, and Cuba. In October 1987 Sankara was murdered and government overthrown in counterrevolutionary military coup by troops loyal to Capt. Blaise Compaoré.

Cambodia – After 1975 victory of liberation forces in Vietnam, neighboring Cambodia's government was overthrown by Khmer Rouge, a murderous Stalinist party headed by Pol Pot. New regime renamed country Democratic Kampuchea and imposed reign of terror on working people, forcing mass evacuation of cities and towns. Driven from power January 1979 by Vietnamese troops and Cambodian opposition forces. Cambodia restored as country's name 1989. *See also:* Vietnam.

Cannon, James P. (1890–1974) – Leader of Communist Party in US from founding in 1919. Member, Executive Committee of Communist International, 1922. Expelled in 1928 for backing world fight led by Leon Trotsky to continue V.I. Lenin's proletarian internationalist course, Cannon was national secretary of Communist League of America and then Socialist Workers Party until 1953; national chairman until 1972. Author of *The Struggle for a Proletarian Party* among many other works.

CIO (Congress of Industrial Organizations) – Established in 1935 as committee of the craft-based American Federation of Labor (AFL) to organize nonunion workers in mass production industries. Became separate industrial union federation in 1936. Through organizing victories by AFL and other unions in 1934 in Minneapolis, San Francisco, and Toledo, and subsequent CIO organizing battles by workers in auto, steel, rubber, and other industries, share of unionized workers increased from

7 percent to 20 percent by 1941. AFL-CIO was formed from merger of two federations in 1955.

Coal strike (1977–78) – Longest nationwide coal strike in US history, with more than 180,000 miners in 22 states walking out December 6, 1977, for 110 days. Coal bosses, seeking to cripple UMWA, sought to impose no-strike pledge, gut union safety committees, institute probation for new hires, eliminate health and pension plans, and introduce "incentive pay" to speed up production. Miners stood firm, defied President James Carter's back-to-work order under Taft-Hartley Act, and won broad working-class solidarity, blocking union-busting drive.

Coalition of Labor Union Women (CLUW) – Founded March 1974 at meeting of more than 3,000 women from 58 international unions, with AFL-CIO backing.

Communist International (Comintern) – Founded by V.I. Lenin and Bolshevik leadership in 1919 as world organization of proletarian parties seeking to emulate October 1917 conquest of state power by workers and peasants in Russia. Reports and resolutions of first four congresses (1919–22) under leadership of Lenin, Trotsky, and other Bolshevik leaders remain program of revolutionary communist parties world over. *See also:* Bolsheviks.

Dobbs, Farrell (1907–1983) – National secretary, Socialist Workers Party 1953–1972 and four-time SWP presidential candidate. Party's national labor secretary, national organization secretary, then national chairman 1940–1953. A leader of union organizing battles in 1930s that forged industrial union movement in US. Part of central leadership that led 1934 strikes that made Minneapolis a union town, and then principal leader of over-the-road organizing drives in 1938–39 that brought quarter million truck drivers into Teamsters across Midwest and Mid-South. Resigned as Teamsters general organizer in 1940 to become SWP labor secretary. In early 1940s he and seventeen other SWP and Teamster leaders were railroaded to federal prison by US rulers for organizing union opposition to Washington's imperialist aims in World War II. *See also:* Smith Act trial.

Economism – Refers to currents in Russian Social Labor Democratic Party in late 1800s and early 1900s seeking to limit working-class movement to economic struggles for better wages and job conditions. Downplayed need for revolutionary workers party and belittled communist theory and working-class political consciousness. V.I. Lenin rebutted Economists' reformist course in 1902 pamphlet *What Is To Be Done?* and other works.

Engels, Frederick (1820–1895) – Founding leader with Karl Marx of modern communist workers movement. Co-author with Marx of Communist Manifesto, late 1847–early 1848. A leader of 1848–49 revolution in Germany and combatant in military resistance to crushing of revolution. Active in International Working Men's Association (1864–76) and, after Marx's death in 1883, central international leader of revolutionary workers movement. *See also:* Marx, Karl.

Equal Rights Amendment (ERA) – Proposed amendment to US Constitution: "Equality of rights under the law shall not be denied or abridged by the United States or by any state on account of sex." Adopted by Congress March 1972 and submitted to state legislatures for ratification. In June 1982 ERA fell three states short of needed 38 by deadline for ratification set by Congress.

Ethiopian Revolution (1974) – Emperor Haile Selassie was overthrown in popular revolution, ending Ethiopia's centuries-long monarchy, based on feudal social relations. New republican government initiated land reform and other antifeudal measures.

Experimental Negotiating Agreement (ENA) – No-strike pact signed in 1973 by the United Steelworkers of America (USWA) officialdom and basic steel corporations. *See also:* Steelworkers Fight Back.

Farmer-Labor Party – Founded in Minnesota in 1918 during First World War by trade unions and farmers groups, with support from urban middle-class layers. Ran candidates against both Democrats and Republicans for state office and Congress but limited its program to capitalist reform. Drawn toward Franklin Roosevelt's Democratic administration during economic and social crisis of 1930s, FLP dissolved into Democratic Party during World War II.

Fourth International – World organization of communist workers parties founded in 1938 at initiative of Bolshevik leader Leon Trotsky in collaboration with Socialist Workers Party leadership and revolutionists in other countries. Its program continued proletarian internationalist course charted by Communist International (Comintern), founded in 1919 under Lenin's leadership. In latter 1920s, after Lenin's death, privileged bureaucratic layers in USSR, whose representative leader was Joseph Stalin, subordinated Comintern to Moscow's diplomatic needs and national interests, imposing class-collaborationist course on affiliated Communist Parties around the world.

Grenada Revolution (1979–83) – Popular revolution that in March 1979 brought to power workers and farmers government in eastern Caribbean island of Grenada. Under Maurice Bishop's leadership, working people threw off US and British imperialist domination and capitalist political rule. In October 1983 government was overthrown in counterrevolution by Stalinist faction headed by Bernard Coard. Bishop, other revolutionary leaders, and workers and youth resisting coup were murdered and 24-hour curfew imposed. Counterrevolution opened door to invasion by Washington, which installed pro-US regime.

Halstead, Fred (1927–1988) – Garment worker and longtime leader of Socialist Workers Party. A national leader of movement against Vietnam War. SWP presidential candidate, 1968. Author *Out Now! A Participant's Account of the Movement in the United States Against the Vietnam War.*

IAM – International Association of Machinists.

Independent truckers – Independent truck owner-operators organized strikes in US in late 1960s and '70s for union recognition,
livable hauling rates, and safety. Capitalist freight-hauling companies, backed by US government, opposed truckers' demands,
declaring them contractors barred from collective bargaining.
Teamsters officials deployed armed goons against these fights
and instructed members to scab on them. For account of how
a class-struggle leadership addressed these fellow workers, see
"How the Teamsters union organized independent truckers in
the 1930s" in *Teamster Politics* by Farrell Dobbs.

Iranian Revolution – In February 1979, US-backed monarchy of
Shah Reza Pahlavi in Iran was overthrown by revolutionary
mobilizations of working people and youth. Protests starting in 1978 culminated in strikes, workplace takeovers, and
other mass protests. Bourgeois forces led by Shiite Muslim
clerics mobilized thugs to attack workers, women demanding rights, Kurds and other oppressed nationalities, and
revolutionary-minded workers organizing a communist party.
Political counterrevolution, widely misnamed "Iranian Revolution," was consolidated by 1983.

Iron Range strike (1977) – During 138-day strike based in northern Minnesota's Iron Range, some 18,000 USWA-organized
iron ore miners shut down two-thirds of US production. They
pushed back mine owners' assault on wages, health, and safety.

Kampuchea – See Cambodia.

Lenin, V.I. (1870–1924) – Central leader of Bolshevik party, which led
workers and peasants to power in world's first socialist revolution in October 1917. Led new Soviet republic. Founding leader
of Communist International, 1919. In last year of political life,
led fight in Russian Communist Party and Communist International to defend proletarian internationalist course against
growing privileged social layers that Joseph Stalin came to represent. *See also:* Bolsheviks, Communist International, Soviets.

Luxemburg, Rosa (1871–1919) – Leader of revolutionary proletarian wing of German Social Democratic Party (SPD). Opposed SPD leadership majority who sought to "reform" capitalism. Fought reformists' patriotic capitulation to Berlin's imperialist war aims in World War I. Hailed Bolshevik Revolution in Russia. Helped lead failed workers revolution in Germany in 1918–1919; killed by thugs of SPD-backed bourgeois regime.

Machinists union – See IAM (International Association of Machinists).

Marx, Karl (1818–1883) – Founding leader with Frederick Engels of modern communist workers movement. Co-author with Engels of Communist Manifesto, late 1847–early 1848. A leader of 1848–49 revolution in Germany. Founder of International Working Men's Association (1864–76), often called First International. Writings of Marx and Engels provide political foundation for proletarian revolutionists worldwide to this day. *See also:* Engels, Frederick.

Milwaukee Road and freight carriers' offensive – Milwaukee Road's owners were among first rail freight carriers in 1970s to cut crew sizes to boost profits. Began bankruptcy proceedings in 1977, announcing thousands of layoffs. Rail workers resisted, demanding "Investigate Milwaukeegate," but bosses and courts protected capital at expense of workers' jobs and safety. With complicity of union officials, rail owners slashed freight crews in later decades from four workers to two, and in some cases to a single engineer.

Miners for Democracy (MFD) – Rank-and-file movement in UMWA founded April 1970. Forged through fights by miners in West Virginia and other Appalachian coalfields against black lung disease, deadly explosions, and other unsafe conditions. After 1969 assassination of its candidate for UMWA president, Joseph Yablonski, MFD in 1972 ousted entrenched bureaucracy of president Tony Boyle, who had collaborated with mine bosses. Arnold Miller was elected UMWA president. Boyle was later convicted of murders of Yablonski and his family. *See also:* Black lung disease.

NEA (National Education Association) – Along with American Federation of Teachers (AFT), one of two major US teachers unions.

Nicaraguan Revolution – On July 19, 1979, Sandinista National Liberation Front led popular insurrection toppling US-backed Somoza family tyranny. FSLN-led workers and peasants government mobilized toilers against landlords and capitalists, defeating US imperialist-inspired counterrevolutionary ("contra") war by 1987. Gave impetus to popular struggles across Central America and forged ties with revolutions in Cuba and Grenada. In late 1980s, as FSLN leadership abandoned revolutionary course, workers and peasants turned away from it. Capitalist social relations were maintained. *See also:* Somoza Debayle, Anastasio.

OCAW – Oil, Chemical and Atomic Workers union. In 2005 became part of United Steelworkers.

Oklahoma City UAW organizing drive – In July 1979 workers at General Motors plant in Oklahoma City voted more than 2–1 to join United Auto Workers (UAW).

OPEIU – Office and Professional Employees International Union.

Perspectiva Mundial – Spanish-language socialist magazine begun January 1977. Merged with *Militant* newsweekly in 2005, becoming section called *El Militante*.

Recession (1974–75) – At the time, longest and deepest contraction of production and trade since Great Depression of 1930s. Jobless rate in US soared to 9 percent.

Right to Vote Committee (UTU) – Committee in United Transportation Union that fought for members' right to ratify contracts with rail bosses. Began 1969 in Chicago local, won support across US and Canada. Right-to-vote motion defeated at 1971 UTU convention.

Sankara, Thomas – *See* Burkina Faso.

Smith Act trial (1941) – In late 1941 eighteen SWP and Minneapolis Teamster leaders were framed for violating Smith Act, a 1940 federal thought-control law. Convicted of "conspiring" to "teach, advocate and encourage" revolutionary ideas, their real "crime" was organizing labor opposition to Washington's aims in World War II. James P. Cannon, Farrell Dobbs, and ten others were imprisoned from December 31, 1943, to early 1945 in Sandstone federal penitentiary in Minnesota. Six others served shorter terms. *See also:* Cannon, James P.; Dobbs, Farrell; Teamster series.

Socialist Workers Party branches, locals, districts – Branches are basic unit of SWP with five or more members. According to SWP constitution, "where three or more branches exist in the same locality," they constitute a local and elect a local executive committee. By decision of party's National Committee, state or district executive committees may be elected to guide party work over larger geographical areas.

Socialist Workers Party National Committee – The party's highest leadership body between conventions, whose delegates elect it. The National Committee elects a Political Committee, which is responsible to it and implements the party's decisions between NC meetings.

Somoza Debayle, Anastasio (1925–1980) – Last of Somoza family dynasty of dictators begun in 1936. Ruled in Nicaragua from mid-1960s until July 1979 revolutionary triumph. Assassinated in Paraguay, 1980.

Soviets – Meaning "councils" in Russian, these delegated bodies emerged during 1905 and 1917 revolutions, elected by workers, peasants, soldiers, and sailors to represent them in struggle. In October 1917, at initiative of Lenin-led Bolsheviks, working people overthrew capitalist Provisional Government and established workers and peasants republic based on soviets. *See also:* Bolsheviks; Lenin, V.I.; Trotsky, Leon.

Spontaneism – View that working-class leadership arises on its own as revolutionary action requires it. Spontaneists reject building proletarian parties along revolutionary centralist lines of Bolsheviks under V.I. Lenin's leadership.

Steelworkers Fight Back – Rank-and-file movement launched 1975 in United Steelworkers under leadership of Ed Sadlowski, president, USWA District 31 (Chicago and northwest Indiana). Sought members' right to strike and vote on contracts. In 1977 Sadlowski ran for USWA president against Lloyd McBride, candidate of union officialdom, which colluded with steel bosses. Sadlowski won in basic steel mills and many smaller shops but was declared by USWA officials to have lost with 42 percent of vote.

Steelworkers Local 8888 (Newport News, Virginia) – Workers at giant Tenneco shipyard struck for nearly three months in early 1979 and won recognition for USWA Local 8888.

Surplus value – Portion of value created by workers during capitalist production that is kept by bourgeoisie as surplus instead of paid to workers as wages. Source of profit, rent, and interest divided among rival industrial, commercial, and financial capitalists through competition.

SWP leadership school – From 1980 to 1986, SWP organized ten sessions of six-month-long leadership school. Focused on political writings of Marx and Engels as they drew lessons of class struggle from 1840s through 1870s and helped lead first communist workers organizations in history. Barnes's report, "Educating the leadership of a proletarian party" (January 1980) is published in *The Changing Face of US Politics*. During opening years of SWP turn, each SWP branch conducted class series on V.I. Lenin's political writings 1902–1917.

Teamsters (International Brotherhood of Teamsters) – Founded 1903, when goods were transported locally by drivers handling teams of horses ("teamsters"). With rise of motorized trucking, drivers were organized on citywide basis along craft union lines. Organizing drives in 1930s brought quarter million over-the-road haulers into Teamsters on industrial union basis. *See also:* Brown, Bill; Teamster series.

Teamster series – *Teamster Rebellion, Teamster Power, Teamster Politics,* and *Teamster Bureaucracy* are four-volume series on 1930s strikes and organizing drives that transformed Teamsters union in Minneapolis and then across Midwest into fighting industrial union movement. Written by Farrell Dobbs, a central leader of these battles and later Socialist Workers Party national secretary. *See also:* Dobbs, Farrell.

Trotsky, Leon (1879–1940) – Part of central Bolshevik leadership under V.I. Lenin that led October 1917 revolution in Russia and Communist International. Commanded Red Army in 1918–20 civil war, which defeated counterrevolutionary troops and imperialist armies. From mid-1920s led worldwide fight to keep Communist International on Lenin's proletarian course, continuing struggle from exile after 1929 deportation from USSR. Founding leader of Fourth International, 1938. Murdered in Mexico on Stalin's orders.

Trotsky School – Six-month educational program for SWP leaders and cadres, held from 1946 to 1963.

UAW – United Auto Workers union.

UMWA – United Mine Workers of America, founded 1890; one of first unions to organize Blacks into membership. Breaking from craft-union-based AFL in mid-1930s, was among founding unions in Congress of Industrial Organizations (CIO).

USWA – United Steelworkers of America.

UTU – United Transportation Union, today called SMART TD. Founded 1969 through merger of four craft unions including firemen, engineers, conductors, brakemen, and switchmen. Since 2008 merger with Sheet Metal Workers' International Association, amalgamated union's rail division took new name.

Vietnam – In 1975 Vietnamese liberation forces defeated US-installed regime in southern half of country and expelled Washington's last troops. They reunified Vietnam, partitioned by French, British, and US imperialism in 1945. In 1979, when Hanoi joined Cambodian opposition to overturn murderous Pol Pot tyranny, Beijing, which backed Pol Pot, invaded Vietnam. While SWP supported overthrow of Pol Pot and condemned Beijing's invasion, most radicals in US and world denounced Vietnam. China's invasion was repelled later in 1979. *See also:* Cambodia.

Wage-price freeze (1971) – In August 1971 Richard Nixon administration declared 90-day wage freeze and sham "price freeze." White House also halted dollar's convertibility to gold. As Vietnam War–fueled inflation eroded dollar reserves of US imperialist rivals, foreign governments, especially France, sought to cash in dollar holdings for gold. By closing US Treasury's gold window and ending dollar's fixed exchange rate, all world currencies became and remain so-called fiat money. None has any labor value or price except relative to others; they are mere ledger notations.

Worker-bolshevik – Originally referred to factory worker cadres of Bolshevik party in Russia under leadership of V.I. Lenin. Term adopted by working-class cadres of communist parties that trace continuity to Bolsheviks and Communist International.

Young Socialist Alliance (YSA) – Founded in 1960 as independent revolutionary youth organization in political solidarity with Socialist Workers Party. Changed name to Young Socialists in 1994.

INDEX

When you've finished *The Turn to Industry,* you'll want to read...

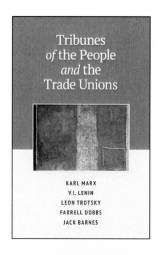

... *Companions to this book*

In Defense of Marxism
LEON TROTSKY
$17. Also in Spanish.

The Struggle for a Proletarian Party
JAMES P. CANNON
$20. Also in Spanish.

Two revolutionary workers leaders record the victorious struggle to keep the communist movement on a proletarian political course in face of growing imperialist pressure during the US buildup to enter World War II. "The class composition of the party," says Trotsky, "must correspond to its class program."

The Communist Manifesto
KARL MARX AND FREDERICK ENGELS

Communism, say the founding leaders of the revolutionary workers movement, is not a set of preconceived principles but workers' line of march to power, springing from a "movement going on under our very eyes." $5. Also in Spanish, French, Farsi, and Arabic.

The Teamster Series

FARRELL DOBBS

From the Midwest strikes and organizing drives in the 1930s that forged a fighting industrial union movement, to the antiwar campaign of class conscious workers resisting the US rulers' profit-driven war aims.

Four books "worth reading, rereading, and reviewing," says Jack Barnes. The more experience workers gain in industry and the unions, "the more we'll get out of those books every time we go back to them."

$16 each. Also in Spanish. *Teamster Rebellion* also in French, Farsi, and Greek.

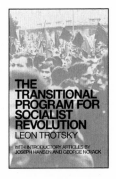

Transitional Program for Socialist Revolution

LEON TROTSKY

The Socialist Workers Party program, drafted by Trotsky in 1938, still guides the SWP and communists the world over today. The party "uncompromisingly gives battle to all political groupings tied to the apron strings of the bourgeoisie. Its task—the abolition of capitalism's domination. Its aim—socialism. Its method— the proletarian revolution." $17

IS SOCIALIST REVOLUTION IN THE US POSSIBLE?

Is Socialist Revolution in the US Possible?

A Necessary Debate
Among Working People

MARY-ALICE WATERS

An unhesitating "Yes"—that's the answer given here. Possible—but not inevitable. That depends on what working people *do*. $7. Also in Spanish, French, and Farsi.

The Clintons' Anti-Working-Class Record

Why Washington Fears Working People

JACK BARNES

What working people need to know about the profit-driven course of Democrats and Republicans alike since the White House of William and Hillary Clinton in the 1990s. And the political awakening of workers seeking to understand and resist the capitalist rulers' assaults. $10. Also in Spanish, French, Farsi, and Greek.

The Eastern Airlines Strike

Accomplishments
of the Rank-and-File Machinists

ERNIE MAILHOT, JUDY STRANAHAN, JACK BARNES

The story of the 686-day strike in which a rank-and-file resistance by airline workers prevented Eastern's union-busting onslaught from becoming the road toward a profitable nonunion company. $7

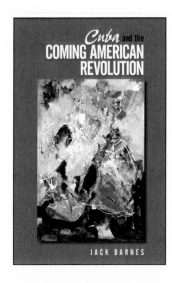

Cuba and the Coming American Revolution

JACK BARNES

This is a book about the struggles of working people in the imperialist heartland, the youth attracted to them, and the example set by the Cuban people that revolution is not only necessary—it can be made. It is about the class struggle in the US, where the revolutionary capacities of workers and farmers are today as utterly discounted by the ruling powers as were those of the Cuban toilers. And just as wrongly. $10. Also in Spanish, French, and Farsi.

Revolutionary Continuity

Marxist Leadership in the United States

FARRELL DOBBS

"Successive generations of proletarian revolutionists have participated in the movements of the working class and its allies and sought to steer them along the correct path.... Marxists today owe them not only homage for their deeds. We also have a duty to learn where they went wrong as well as what they did right so their errors are not repeated."—Farrell Dobbs
Two volumes: *The Early Years, 1848–1917*, $17; *Birth of the Communist Movement, 1918–1922*, $17.

"It's the Poor Who Face the Savagery of the US 'Justice' System"

The Cuban Five Talk about Their Lives within the US Working Class

How US cops, courts, and prisons work as "an enormous machine for grinding people up." Five Cuban revolutionaries framed up and held in US jails for 16 years explain the human devastation of capitalist "justice"—and how socialist Cuba is different. $10. Also in Spanish, Farsi, and Greek.

REVOLUTIONARY LEADERS IN THEIR OWN WORDS

February 1965: The Final Speeches Malcolm X

Our revolt is not "simply a racial conflict of Black against white, or a purely American problem. Rather, we are seeing a global rebellion of the oppressed against the oppressor, the exploited against the exploiter." Speeches and interviews from the last three weeks of Malcolm X's life. $17

Lenin's Final Fight

Speeches and Writings, 1922–23

V.I. LENIN

In 1922 and 1923, V.I. Lenin, central leader of the world's first socialist revolution, waged what was to be his last political battle—one that was lost following his death. At stake was whether that revolution, and the international communist movement it led, would remain on the revolutionary proletarian course that had brought workers and peasants to power in October 1917. $17. Also in Spanish, Farsi, and Greek.

Maurice Bishop Speaks

The Grenada Revolution and Its Overthrow, 1979–83

The triumph of the 1979 revolution in the Caribbean island of Grenada under the leadership of Maurice Bishop gave hope to millions throughout the Americas. Invaluable lessons from the workers and farmers government destroyed by a Stalinist-led coup in 1983. $20

Socialism and Man in Cuba

ERNESTO CHE GUEVARA,
FIDEL CASTRO

One of the most profound revolutionary documents ever written. "Man truly reaches his full human condition when he produces without being compelled by physical necessity to sell himself as a commodity." —Ernesto Che Guevara, 1965. $5. Also in Spanish, French, Farsi, and Greek.

In Defense of Socialism

Four Speeches on the 30th Anniversary of the Cuban Revolution, 1988–89

FIDEL CASTRO

$12. Also in Greek.

We Are Heirs of the World's Revolutions

Speeches from the Burkina Faso Revolution, 1983–87

THOMAS SANKARA

How peasants and workers in this West African country established a popular revolutionary government and began to fight hunger, illiteracy, and economic backwardness imposed by imperialist domination. They set an example not only for workers and small farmers in Africa, but their class brothers and sisters the world over. $10. Also in Spanish, French, and Farsi.

Puerto Rico: Independence Is a Necessity

RAFAEL CANCEL MIRANDA

One of the five Puerto Rican Nationalists imprisoned by Washington for more than 25 years and released in 1979 speaks out on the brutal reality of US colonial domination, the example of Cuba's socialist revolution, and the ongoing struggle for independence. $5. Also in Spanish and Farsi.

Women in Cuba
The making of a revolution
within the revolution

From Santiago de Cuba and the Rebel Army,
to the birth of the Federation of Cuban Women

Vilma Espín
Asela de los Santos
Yolanda Ferrer

Women in Cuba: The Making of a Revolution Within the Revolution

VILMA ESPÍN, ASELA DE LOS SANTOS, YOLANDA FERRER

The integration of women into the ranks and leadership of the Cuban Revolution was inseparably intertwined with the proletarian course of the revolution from its very first actions. This is the story of that revolution and how it transformed the women and men who made it. $17. Also in Spanish and Greek.

Cosmetics, Fashions, and the Exploitation of Women

JOSEPH HANSEN, EVELYN REED, MARY-ALICE WATERS

How big business plays on women's second-class status in class society and what Reed calls "capitalist social compulsion" to market cosmetics and rake in profits. And how the entry of millions of women into the workforce has irreversibly changed relations between women and men—for the better. $12. Also in Spanish and Farsi.

Art and Revolution

Writings on Literature, Politics, and Culture

LEON TROTSKY

"Art can become a strong ally of revolution only insofar as it remains faithful to itself," wrote Trotsky in 1938. $15

The Long View of History

GEORGE NOVACK

Why and how the revolutionary struggle by working people to end oppression and exploitation is a realistic perspective. $5. Also in Farsi.

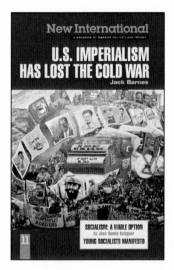

PATHFINDER AROUND THE WORLD

Visit our website for a complete list of titles and to place orders

www.pathfinderpress.com

PATHFINDER DISTRIBUTORS

UNITED STATES
(and Caribbean, Latin America, and East Asia)
> *Pathfinder Books, 306 W. 37th St., 13th Floor*
> *New York, NY 10018*

CANADA
> *Pathfinder Books, 7107 St. Denis, Suite 204*
> *Montreal, QC H2S 2S5*

UNITED KINGDOM
(and Europe, Africa, Middle East, and South Asia)
> *Pathfinder Books, 5 Norman Rd.*
> *Seven Sisters, London N15 4ND*

AUSTRALIA
(and Southeast Asia and the Pacific)
> *Pathfinder Books, Suite 22, 10 Bridge St.*
> *Granville, Sydney, NSW 2142*

NEW ZEALAND
> *Pathfinder Books, 188a Onehunga Mall Rd., Onehunga, Auckland 1061*
> *Postal address: P.O. Box 13857, Auckland 1643*